THE CROSSROADS COOKBOOK
A Star Original

Meg Mortimer and the staff of the Crossroads Motel bring you a different three-course menu for each week of the year. The recipes are designed to make the best use of seasonal fresh foods, and they are full of hints and advice from Meg's experienced chefs that will give your cooking the professional touch. There are good English dishes, favourites from all over Europe, and more exotic recipes that Meg and her staff have brought back from places like Mexico, Tunisia and Jamaica.

Try Tabouleh, Baked Mackerel with Gooseberry Sauce, Mexican Scallops, Baked Caribbean Bananas, Chakchouka, Honey-glazed Gammon, Green Figs in Pernod, Sole with Grapes and Cheese Sauce and Sailor's Duff. They're all delicious!

GW00393414

THE CROSSROADS
COOKBOOK

Hazel Adair and Peter Ling

A STAR BOOK
published by
the Paperback Division of
W. H. ALLEN & Co. Ltd

A Star Book
Published in 1977
by the Paperback Division of
W. H. Allen & Co. Ltd
A Howard and Wyndham Company
44 Hill Street, London W1X 8LB

Copyright © 1977 by Hazel Adair and Peter Ling

Printed in Great Britain by
Hazell Watson & Viney Ltd, Aylesbury, Bucks

ISBN 0 352 39561 3

PRODUCED BY ARRANGEMENT WITH ATV LIMITED
—
THIS IS A LESLIE FREWIN IMPAC BOOK
FOR
STAR BOOKS

WELCOME——

... to the kitchens of the Crossroads Motel.

At the latest count, nearly twenty million people, in Great Britain alone, switch on their television sets four times a week, to watch *Crossroads* .... And you'd be surprised how many of these millions take the time and trouble to write in and tell us what they like about the programme – and what they don't like as well!

Some eager young ladies even write in to apply for jobs as waitresses or washers-up at the Motel; recently we seem to have had staffing problems in the Motel office, and a lot of girls have volunteered to come and take over as secretary to Meg and David. But even more people write in to tell us how much they wish they could take a holiday and stay at Crossroads as guests – to chat to Jane and Vera and Sandy and all their other old friends, and to eat (in the restaurant or cafeteria) dishes expertly prepared in the Motel kitchens.

Now, at last, here is one way to make some of those wishes come true, as this book brings our very own menus within everybody's range. You can try out the various special recipes, acquire some professional tips from the Motel chefs, and perhaps even pick up some new scraps of gossip from the kitchen staff at the same time!

First – and most important of all – the menus.

From time to time, you've probably seen one of the chefs coming into Meg's sitting-room or David's office, so that the menus can be checked and approved; in the Crossroads restaurant the menu is changed weekly, according to the raw materials available through the changing seasons. So here are the menus for a full year – and in the following pages you will find recipes taking you right from Spring to the following winter; fifty-two weeks of three-course meals for you to try at home. Unless it is stated otherwise, the menus are for four people.

MENUS FOR SPRING

Whitebait
Chicken Portugaise
Apple Souffle Pie

WHITEBAIT
A popular 'easy to prepare' starter which was put on the Crossroads menu by Mr Lovejoy when he first came to the Motel.

½ lb whitebait	**For Garnish:**
1 oz plain flour	lemon wedges
salt and pepper	parsley
juice of 1 lemon	paprika

Wash the whitebait under cold water then dry with a cloth. Toss them in flour seasoned with salt and pepper. Put in a frying basket and shake off surplus flour. Plunge the basket into deep, very hot fat or oil. Cook for 3½ minutes. Drain fish on crumpled greaseproof paper and sprinkle with lemon juice and paprika.
Put the fish in a pile on a serving dish and garnish with parsley and lemon wedges.

CHICKEN PORTUGAISE
Over the years, people from almost every country in the world have passed through the swinging doors into Crossroads reception – but as far as anyone can remember, the Motel has never had a Portuguese guest. . . . Except for this – a Portuguese chicken dish that entered the menus as a visitor, and became such a firm favourite, it stayed on to become a welcome 'regular'.

7

4 chicken joints (or a small chicken, quartered)	1 lemon
butter	a cupful of rice
8 small onions	1 tumbler of white wine
2 cloves of garlic, 1 bay leaf	salt and pepper

An earthenware casserole or stewpot is ideal for this, because it needs to cook slowly and gently. Skin the chicken joints (once you get the knack, it's quite easy; you can pull the skin off in one piece by pulling it inside out, rather like peeling off a rubber glove) and smear generously with butter, then place in the casserole. Peel the onions – if you can't get small ones, cut them in half – and then pack them into the spaces around the chicken. Grate the lemon rind and sprinkle it over, then cut the lemon in half and squeeze it, adding the juice to the casserole, together with the crushed cloves of garlic, the bay leaf and the rice. Season lightly and pour the wine over the whole lot. Put on a well-fitting lid and cook for two hours or more (330 F, Gas mark 2).

APPLE SOUFFLE PIE

8 oz short crust pastry	½ saltspoon freshly grated nutmeg
1 heaped tablespoon flour	
3 oz castor sugar	1½ oz butter
4 oz brown sugar (soft)	8 cooking apples
1 saltspoon cinnamon	juice of half a small lemon
a pinch of salt	2 tablespoons double cream

Mix the sugars, flour and seasonings in a bowl. Rub in the butter.

Peel, core and slice the apples, then sprinkle with lemon juice. Add three quarters of the sugar mixture and coat the apple slices evenly with it.

Line pie plate or flan dish with the pastry and fill with the apples. Cover with remaining sugar and flour mixture. Bake in a hot oven (450 F, Gas mark 8) for 10 minutes then reduce to 375 F, Gas mark 5 and continue baking for 25 minutes so that apples are just cooked.

Pour cream over pie and cook for a further 10 minutes. Serve straight from oven.

Grapefruit with Prawns
Crown Roast of Lamb
Chocolate Mousse

GRAPEFRUIT WITH PRAWNS

Here's something really unusual – you might not think these two strong flavours would go well together, but they do.

2 *grapefruits*	1 *small carton of soured*
5 *oz peeled prawns*	*cream*
3 *tablespoons of*	*paprika pepper for*
mayonnaise	*garnishing*

Cut the grapefruits in halves, and carefully run a pointed knife round the inside of the skin, then criss-cross along the lines of the segments until you can scoop them out, leaving the half-shells empty. (Trim away any remaining bits of pith.)

Strain off any extra juice (and drink it! – very good for the complexion, according to Vera Downend). Mix the segments with the prawns, then refill the shells with this mixture. Now combine the mayonnaise and soured cream, and pour it over as a dressing, topping off each one with a dash of paprika pepper.

CROWN ROAST OF LAMB

For this attractive dish you need a whole loin or best end of neck of lamb. Ask your butcher to chine it and chop the ribs to equal lengths. The upper portions of the bones must then be trimmed and scraped and each chop is cut through almost to the skin. The joints are now folded inside out and fastened together by sewing or tying to form a crown.

The hole in the centre must now be stuffed. At Crossroads we use the minced trimmings of the lamb, white breadcrumbs, chopped parsley, grated lemon rind and a little powdered rosemary, the whole being dampened with red wine and well seasoned with pepper and salt.

Place into a baking dish spread with butter or dripping, cover 'crown' bones with foil to prevent burning and cook at 375 F, Gas mark 5 allowing 25 minutes per pound. Test to see if the joint is cooked before serving as the stuffing absorbs a lot of the heat. Serve on a bed of vegetables with a small cutlet frill on each bone.

CHOCOLATE MOUSSE

Mr Lovejoy says that after a lifetime of sampling and experimenting with a hundred different ways of making a chocolate mousse – this is the one-and-only altogether incomparable winner! And when Mr Lovejoy makes a pronouncement like that, nobody argues. Come to think of it – nobody who ever tasted this recipe would want to argue anyway.

½ lb block of plain chocolate	3 eggs
	rum or vanilla essence to
1 small coffee-cup of black coffee	flavour
	whipped cream for
½ oz butter	decoration

Break up the chocolate in a small pan and pour in the coffee, then heat through gently, stirring as it melts, until it is smoothly blended. Add the butter and let it melt, then the yolks of the eggs, stirring them in one at a time; finally a few drops of rum or vanilla.

Now whisk the egg-whites until they are stiff. Turn the chocolate mixture into a large bowl, and then fold in the egg-whites until they are thoroughly absorbed. (If you try to cut a corner by mixing the chocolate into the egg-whites, it doesn't blend properly, for some reason.) Pour it into small

10

dishes or dessert glasses and leave overnight in the fridge to set.

Decorate before serving with swirls of whipped cream.

Pate Maison
Chicken with Prawn & Mushroom
Oriental Ambrosia

PATE MAISON

This smooth 'Pate Maison' is a favourite all the year round, and has the advantage of keeping well. The recipe will make several pots full, which can stand at the back of the fridge until they're wanted. (Incidentally, a small earthenware crock of pate makes an unusual and rich Christmas gift for 'the man who has everything'!)

¾ lb chicken livers (persuade your butcher to save them for you)
6 oz butter and 1 oz butter

1 onion
1 clove of garlic, herbs to taste, salt and pepper
3 tablespoons of brandy

Chop the onion and garlic finely and fry them together in the 1 oz of butter until they're just 'coloured'. Add all the other ingredients except the brandy and the butter and continue to fry for two or three minutes. Now either chop very finely, pass through a sieve, or (as in the Motel kitchen) blend in a liquidiser, adding the well-creamed 6 oz of butter and mix all together to a smooth paste. At the last moment, stir in the brandy, then spoon the mixture into china or earthenware pots and leave to cool. Smooth over the tops, and seal them with a thin layer of clarified butter.

CHICKEN WITH PRAWN AND MUSHROOM

Vera Downend sometimes complains that, living alone on the narrowboat, she can't be bothered to cook anything fancy just for herself. Consequently, on the rare occasions

11

when she feels like breaking out and treating herself to supper at the Motel (or even better, when somebody else is paying!) she likes to order something very fancy indeed. And – as she rightly says – 'they don't come much fancier than this'.

4 *chicken joints*	1 *oz flour*
2 *oz peeled prawns*	1 *pint water*
2 *oz button mushrooms*	1 *tablespoon sherry*
2 *carrots*	*lemon juice*
1 *small onion*	1 *bay leaf, salt and pepper*
1 *oz butter*	

Peel and slice the onion and carrots, and put them in a saucepan with the chicken joints, bay leaf, seasoning and water. Let it boil, then put on the lid and simmer for three quarters of an hour. Take the chicken joints out, let them cool sufficiently to be able to remove all the skin and bone, then arrange the meat in a casserole and keep in a hot place. Put all the skin and bone back in the saucepan and carry on simmering for another half hour, then strain this stock into a jug.

Meanwhile, wash and slice the mushrooms and cook them in butter, with a dash of lemon juice, salt and pepper. Remove the mushrooms, sprinkle in the flour and cook for a few minutes, stirring all the time; then blend in half a pint of the stock. Bring to the boil and simmer for a few more minutes. Now take the pan from the heat, stir in the sherry, prawns and mushrooms, and adjust the seasoning. Pour this sauce over the chicken in the casserole, and serve.

ORIENTAL AMBROSIA
. . . But of course Vera doesn't always live alone! While she had her son, Clive, staying on the boat, this dessert was a firm favourite.

13 oz tin pineapple titbits
10 oz tin mandarin orange
   segments

⅓ pint sour cream or plain
   yoghourt
a good pinch of salt
3 oz flaked coconut

Drain the fruit thoroughly. Toss all the ingredients together lightly and serve at once.

Coquilles St Jacques
Spiced Steak
Mandarin Whip

COQUILLES ST JACQUES

There are so many ways of serving scallops – and each and every one claims to be the one-and-only classic method! But here is one which many of the Crossroads diners enjoy; it makes a wonderful first course but, if you prefer, you could double the quantities and serve it as a main dish.

4 scallops
¼ lb mushrooms
1 glass white wine
squeeze of lemon juice

1 oz butter
1 small carton of cream
1 oz grated cheese
salt and pepper

Poach the scallops in the wine and lemon juice for a few minutes. When they are cooked, lift out the scallops, let them cool, and then cut them into slices. Now slice up the mushrooms and saute them in butter in another pan, adding the liquor from the first saucepan as soon as they are soft. Stir until the mixture simmers, and then cook rapidly for four or five minutes, then pour in the cream. Now add the sliced scallops to heat through, adding seasoning, then divide up into equal portions in the deep half-shells (if your fishmonger is kind enough to let you have them – otherwise shallow fireproof dishes will have to do!) Sprinkle grated cheese over the top of each one, and brown under the grill.

SPICED STEAK

Nutmeg is a funny thing. (When Sandy was a lot younger, with a schoolboy sense of humour, he used to think it was uproariously comic to say to his mother 'You're a nutmeg' – but that's another story.) The most underrated of spices, often dismissed as 'that stuff you sprinkle on milk puddings', it has a wonderful flavour all its own – and it's the making of this particular recipe.

1 *lb steak*	½ *teaspoon grated nutmeg*
2 *tablespoons dripping*	*salt and pepper*
1 *onion*	*a little beefstock*
½ *bay leaf*	

Beat the steak to tenderise it, cut into four portions, and season with salt and pepper. Fry in the dripping in a heavy oven dish until the meat browns on both sides, then add sliced onion, bay leaf and nutmeg. Pour over a little extra stock so that the meat won't dry out during cooking, put a lid on and let it cook slowly – either in the oven (325 F, Gas mark 3) or over a low flame on top of the stove.

MANDARIN WHIP

Bernard Booth doesn't approve of his cousin Tina Webb's taste in most things but he does approve of this recipe for Mandarin Whip – and so do the Crossroads customers. One of the beauties of this dish is that it can be simply adapted for almost any fruit.

½ *packet tangerine jelly*	**For decoration:**
¼ *pint water, fruit juice*	*whipped cream*
or syrup from tinned fruit	*a few pieces of mandarins*
small tin of mandarin	
orange segments	
8 *fluid oz evaporated milk*	

Dissolve jelly in boiling liquid and leave until cold but not set.

Whip evaporated milk then gradually whip the jelly into it. (NB If the jelly is warm the mixture will separate.) Continue whipping until the mixture thickens, then add chopped fruit and mix quickly and thoroughly. It should be quite thick before pouring into sundae glasses. Keep stirring between filling the glasses.

Leave until set then decorate with piped whipped cream and well drained fruit.

Tuna Stuffed Eggs
Shish Kebabs with Rice Pilaf
Mocha Flan

TUNA STUFFED EGGS

One of our regular standbys! Easy to prepare with ingredients always to hand, this starter proved a godsend when the Motel had a major power cut and some of their fresh food was no longer up to the standard they insist on at Crossroads.

6 eggs
1 7½ oz can tuna fish
2 tablespoons capers
2 teaspoons lemon juice
salt and pepper

½ pint thick mayonnaise
1 tablespoon Dijon mustard
fresh lettuce leaves to
garnish

Cool hardboiled eggs under cold running water and shell them. Cut in half lengthwise and scoop out yolks. Rub them through a fine sieve. Mash tuna fish as finely as possible with a fork and stir in capers. Season with salt and pepper. Having blended the mayonnaise with the Dijon mustard fold three or four tablespoons into the tuna mixture, with a quarter of the sieved egg yolks. Correct seasoning with salt, pepper and lemon juice and pile the whole mixture into the empty egg whites. Arrange the eggs on a bed of lettuce leaves and spoon

over the top of each some mayonnaise topped with the remaining egg yolks to garnish.
Serves 4-6.

SHISH KEBABS WITH RICE PILAF
After his trip to Turkey with Kelly, David Hunter should be an expert on the subject of kebabs (and, let's face it, pretty well everything else. . . . As David says, travel with Kelly really was mind-broadening.) And he's never complained yet about the Crossroads version of this mouth-watering dish from the Eastern Mediterranean.

1 *lb neck fillet of lamb or pork tenderloin or beefsteak*	1 *bay leaf*
	salt, pepper, and a little cooking oil
4 *rashers streaky bacon*	
1 *small onion*	**For the pilaf:**
¼ *lb mushrooms* (*preferably the button kind*)	½ *lb long-grain rice*
	1 *onion*
1 *green pepper*	2 *oz butter*
4 *tomatoes*	1 *tin tomato juice*

You will need four long skewers for this, as you assemble on each one a row of varied titbits. Cut the meat into small cubes, and the rashers into squares of similar size. Quarter the onion, and separate into 'leaves'. Wash and quarter the tomatoes; wash the mushrooms and (if they're small enough) leave whole, or if they're too big, cut them down to size. Wash, de-seed and cut up the pepper into pieces comparable to the onion leaves. Now make up your skewers, varying the ingredients turn and turn about as you go. When they are complete, place in your grill-pan, brush with oil generously, and sprinkle with salt, pepper and crushed bay leaf.
Meanwhile, cook the pilaf, using the method given in the recipe for 'Seafood Risotto' on page 65. (Better do this first, since the kebabs will grill pretty quickly.) Place the pan

16

under the grill and cook for about five to ten minutes, until the kebabs are done, turning occasionally to make sure they cook equally on all sides. Now dish up the pilaf and serve together.

MOCHA FLAN
A popular dish on the Crossroads menus is Mocha Flan. Bernard Booth says the better the coffee is, the better the flan – but instant coffee will do as long as it is strong.

5 oz sweet short crust pastry	¾ pint milk
¼ pint strong coffee	packet chocolate blancmange powder
2 oz sugar	1 orange

Roll out pastry, line a flan case and bake 'blind' in a hot oven until crisp (450 F, Gas mark 8).
Prepare filling by blending the blancmange powder with the cold coffee. Pour boiling milk over this mixture and, having added the sugar and grated orange rind, cook until you have a smooth, thick sauce.
Pour into the prepared flan case and serve hot, decorated with peeled orange segments.

Egg & Prawn Mayonnaise
Spanish Cutlets
Lemon Sorbet

EGG AND PRAWN MAYONNAISE
A welcome change, if you suddenly get bored with straight-forward egg mayonnaise. . . .

4 hard-boiled eggs	1 level teaspoon of curry powder
3 heaped tablespoons of mayonnaise	3 oz shelled prawns
1 small carton of soured cream	paprika pepper and lettuce leaves, for the garnish

17

Remove the eggshells carefully and leave the eggs in cold water while you mix together the mayonnaise, soured cream and curry powder. If you can spare the time, this mixture should be left in the fridge for an hour or so – it thickens up, and it also seems to bring out the flavour.

Then cut the eggs in half longways, (if you use a wet knife, it's easier to slice them cleanly) and arrange the eight halves in a star shape, flat side down, on a bed of lettuce leaves. Heap the shelled prawns into the centre of the star, and spoon the chilled sauce over the whole thing – then sprinkle with paprika pepper to give a dash of colour.

SPANISH CUTLETS

This is a legacy from the dear departed Carlos Rafael; though whether it's an authentic Spanish recipe, or whether Carlos concocted an Anglo-Spanish version to appeal to stay-at-home diners, no-one will ever know. Either way, it's very popular, and a regular in the Crossroads menus.

2 *tablespoons cooking oil*	8 *chipolata sausages*
4 *lamb cutlets*	1 *lb tomatoes*
1 *rasher bacon*	*salt and pepper*

Trim the fat from the cutlets and fry them in oil, then transfer to a casserole and add salt and pepper. Now fry the sliced onion and bacon in the same oil, and when the onion is golden, add the tomatoes (peeled and sliced) and cook for another five minutes. Remove the bacon and chop it finely, then add all these ingredients to the casserole, put on the lid, and cook in a moderate oven (350 F, Gas mark 4) for half an hour.

Grill the chipolatas separately, adding them to the casserole just before you dish up.

LEMON SORBET

Probably the most refreshing of all sweets for a warm day; and it's so light that even guests who feel they've eaten too much already somehow manage to find room for it. Best of all, it's not hard to make, as long as you're careful not to make it over-sweet – if you use too much sugar, it won't freeze properly.

1 *pint water*	*rind and juice of* 4 *lemons*
8 *oz sugar*	2 *egg whites*

With a potato-peeler, cut the rinds off the lemons; then slice the lemons in half and squeeze out the juice. Put the lemon rinds into a pan with the water and sugar; stir until the sugar dissolves over a gentle heat, then bring to the boil for five or six minutes. Let it cool again, and stir in the lemon juice. Strain and freeze.

After about an hour, when the sorbet has half set, turn it out into a chilled bowl and beat with an egg-whisk, folding in the stiffly-beaten egg-whites. Return the mixture to the freezer for at least another hour, stirring once or twice during this time to make sure that it freezes evenly.

Oeufs Florentine
Stuffed Best End of Lamb
Mandarin Flan

OEUFS FLORENTINE

The Rev. Peter Hope's wife, Marilyn, often used to prepare the following dish for her husband's supper. She said that many times he came home after a busy day 'too tired to eat'. This never failed to get his appetite back. But it makes a good starter too, if you leave out the spaghetti.

8 *oz spaghetti*	1 *tablespoon cooking oil*
2 *lbs fresh or* 12 *oz frozen*	2 *good pinches of nutmeg*
spinach	*salt and pepper*
4 *eggs*	⅓ *pint cheese sauce*
2 *oz butter*	

Cook the spaghetti in plenty of well salted boiling water until tender. Drain and stir in 1 oz butter.

If using fresh spinach, wash well. Cook, drain and chop. Sprinkle with nutmeg and a little finely ground pepper.

Arrange the spaghetti on a hot serving dish and top with a layer of spinach.

Place the eggs, poached, on the spinach and mask with cheese sauce.

Grill for a few moments until nicely browned, and serve hot.

STUFFED BEST END OF LAMB

Perhaps this can't claim to be a 'traditional' dish from the Midlands – but Amy Turtle insists that she can remember her grandma cooking it for Sunday dinner . . . and you can't get much more traditional than that!

1 lb or more of boned best end of lamb

For the stuffing:
1 *tablespoonful chopped onion*
½ *oz butter*
rind and juice of half an orange
2½ *tablespoons of breadcrumbs*
2 *teaspoons of mixed herbs*
1 *egg*
salt and pepper

For the sauce:
1 *tablespoon dripping*
1 *level tablespoon of flour*
½ *pint stock*
1 *tablespoon chopped onion*
rind and juice of half an orange
1 *tablespoon of redcurrant jelly*

Fry one tablespoonful of onion in butter until it is soft; then add half the breadcrumbs, herbs, orange juice and rind. Mix and add salt and pepper; spread the mixture on the meat, roll it up and tie – not too tightly. Toss the joint in seasoned flour, then coat with the beaten egg and the remaining breadcrumbs. Roast at 400 F, Gas mark 6 for 45-60 minutes.

To make the sauce, cook chopped onion in dripping, then stir in the flour; add the stock, a little at a time, and red-currant jelly with grated orange rind. Stir until it boils and thickens; add the orange juice, and serve.

MANDARIN FLAN

Facilities for cooking are a little limited in Vera's narrow-boat; as she says, you really need elbow-room to go in for fancy catering! But here's a simple sweet which she can make in a very short time – and for some reason it has proved to be particularly popular with a certain guest of hers who was serving in the Merchant Navy.

1 *sponge flan-base* (*bought ready-made*)
½ *packet of orange or mandarin jelly*

small tin evaporated milk
small tin mandarin oranges
whipped cream for decoration

First dissolve the jelly in ¼ pint of juice from the tin of mandarins. (You can always keep the other half of the jelly for another occasion.) When it has cooled, whisk in the evaporated milk – preferably after it has been kept in the fridge to chill. Now take half the oranges; chop them finely and stir into the mixture. Pour it into the flan and leave to set. When it is firm, decorate with the remaining mandarins, in a circle round the edge, alternating with swirls or rosettes of whipped cream.

Shrimp Fritters
Imperial Chicken
Rhubarb Crunch

SHRIMP FRITTERS

The following recipe comes from Tish Hope. The fritters she makes not only for a hot first course but also as canapes when she and Ted entertain friends to drinks.

21

8 oz peeled shrimps or	5 oz flour
prawns	3 eggs
½ pint water	white pepper
2 oz butter	juice of half a lemon
a good pinch salt	1 teaspoon curry powder

Put water, butter and salt into a medium sized saucepan and bring to the boil. When boiling stir in the flour with a wooden spoon and keep stirring until the paste leaves the sides of the pan clean.

Cool, then add the eggs, one at a time, stirring until all are absorbed.

Add drained shrimps, pepper, curry powder and lemon juice.

With a spoon take large walnut-sized pieces and fry in hot but not boiling fat. Cook on a high flame until the fritters are nicely shaped, dry and golden brown.

Dry on kitchen paper and serve on napkin covered dish.

These are equally delicious made in a batter instead of puff pastry.

For the batter:	2 tablespoons warm water
1½ tablespoons flour	1 egg white
½ tablespoon olive oil	salt

Make the batter by mixing the flour, salt and oil together. Add the warm water and beat into a smooth paste then fold in the stiffly beaten egg white. Dip the shrimps or prawns into the mixture and see that they are well covered. Fry in deep fat until they are brown all over and drain on kitchen paper.

IMPERIAL CHICKEN

As any friends of the Crossroads kitchen will know, Mr McFee claims to be a very well-travelled man who – in his seafaring days – circled the globe countless times. The fact that the only ship he's ever actually known to have sailed in was the old Greenock ferry is neither here nor there; if he hadn't been to St Petersburg – oh, all right then, Leningrad, if you insist – how else could he possibly have collected this recipe which (he swears) was once a favourite in the Imperial Russian Court, long, long ago?

1 *packet demi-sel cheese*	6 *sticks of celery*
1 *carton cottage cheese*	1 *tablespoon olive oil*
½ *teaspoon dried fennel*	1 *glass of white wine*
6 *leeks*	3 *tablespoons brandy*
4 *small carrots*	1 *chicken*
1 *green pepper*	*salt and pepper*

Mix the two kinds of cheese with the fennel, and use this to stuff the chicken. Put the bird into an oven dish, rub salt and pepper into the skin to make it roast crisply, and cook in a hot oven (425 F, Gas mark 7) for twenty minutes.

Now wash and slice all the vegetables very finely, and arrange these round the chicken, then pour the oil and wine (beaten up together) over the whole lot, and cook for another hour.

The last stage is the spectacular one. Put the brandy into a deep ladle and warm it over a low heat, then set it alight and pour the flaming brandy over the chicken. Continue to roast for ten minutes, basting with the liquid in the oven-dish – and bring to the table.

RHUBARB CRUNCH
'What a load of people!' as the rhubarb was heard to say: like the gooseberry, rhubarb is particularly English. Nothing can be nicer than young rhubarb, fresh from the garden, plainly stewed with a little lemon rind for flavour and plenty of sugar. This is Shughie McFee's way of cooking the rhubarb which Carney grows so carefully for Crossroads customers.

4 *oz flour*	1 *oz flour*
5 *oz castor sugar*	¾ *teaspoon baking powder*
4 *oz butter or margarine*	½ *saltspoon salt*
2 *eggs*	*about* 1 *lb cut rhubarb*
10 *oz granulated sugar*	

Preheat oven to 350 F, Gas mark 4. Mix flour, castor sugar and butter or margarine and put into 9″ baking pan. Bake in oven for fifteen minutes. Beat eggs, add granulated sugar, flour, baking powder, salt and rhubarb cut into 1½″ pieces. Pour over other mixture and bake for 30-35 minutes. Keep pan covered with greaseproof or foil to prevent it hardening too much.

Tortilla (*Spanish Omelette*)
Smoked Cod and Sweetcorn
Lemon Ice Cake

TORTILLA (SPANISH OMELETTE)

Another recipe Carlos introduced to Crossroads. This is not the complicated dish that so many tourists to Spain imagine. In fact it is simple and quick to turn out. Usually it is served piping hot as a starter but it can also be eaten cold with salad as a change. Meg used to find that slices of tortilla made a change from sandwiches for Sandy and Jill to take to school for their lunch.

2 *oz diced cooked ham*	4 *eggs*
4 *oz raw potato* (*cut into* *cubes*)	*salt and pepper*
	oil
2 *oz Spanish onion* (*chopped*)	

Heat 1 tablespoon oil in 6″ omelette pan. Add ham, onion and potato cubes and saute gently until cooked (about 10 mins). In a bowl whisk the eggs until well blended and season with salt and pepper. Pour one third of the egg mixture into the pan and cook over a moderate heat, making sure the mixture runs evenly over the pan by lifting the sides of omelette to let the liquid run underneath. Add the remaining egg and cook until a golden crust has formed underneath. Place a large plate over the top of the pan and turn the omelette out upside down. Making sure the pan is clean, add more olive oil and carefully slide the omelette back into the pan to brown on the other side. Slip out on to a hot plate and serve immediately.

SMOKED COD AND SWEETCORN

A special favourite with the younger generation. Glenda Brownlow sampled it and said: 'If fish is brainfood – this could have got me through my school exams!'

1½ *lb smoked cod*	*a little butter*
1 *large tin of sweetcorn*	*salt, pepper and paprika*
¼ *pint single cream*	

Make a layer of tinned sweetcorn at the bottom of a buttered oven-proof dish. Remove any skin and bones from the smoked cod, and cut the fish into small pieces, laying them on top of the corn. Dot with butter and seasoning; add another layer of corn, and then more cod, continuing until it's all used up. Then pour the cream over the top, and bake (at 350 F, Gas mark 4) until the fish is cooked through – about an hour. Sprinkle on paprika and serve. It's at its best with an accompaniment of broccoli – and because of the sweetcorn, you won't need any potatoes.

LEMON ICE CAKE

Puddings that are frozen instead of cooked are always popular – not only with guests, but also with the chefs. (Somehow toiling over a cold fridge isn't nearly as arduous as slaving over a hot stove.) The only thing about it is that you will need to make up your mind in advance when you are going to want this dessert – because it has to be made the day before and left in the fridge overnight.

4 *oz butter*	18 *sponge fingers*
6 *oz castor sugar*	*whipped cream*
4 *eggs*	1 *lemon*

Separate the yolks from the whites of the eggs. Cream the butter and sugar together and beat in the egg-yolks with the grated rind and juice of the lemon. Then beat the whites stiffly and fold them into the mixture.

Line an oblong cake tin with the sponge fingers, each one split longways into two or even three. Fill the tin with a layer of lemon mixture, then a layer of sponge fingers, another of lemon, and so on, finishing with a 'lid' of sponge fingers. Cover tightly with tinfoil, and chill overnight. When you dish it up, turn it out on a plate and cut into slices, serving each one with a spoonful of whipped cream.

Spring Soup
Chicken Maryland
Creme Brulee

SPRING SOUP

Carney's best vegetables go to the making of this soup – a best-seller on the Crossroads menu.

2 *quarts of water with 2 bouillon cubes*	12 *stalks of fresh asparagus cut into one inch pieces*
3 *tablespoons butter*	**or** 10 *oz frozen asparagus, thawed*
1 *large carrot thinly sliced*	
3 *potatoes peeled and thinly sliced*	10 *oz frozen chopped spinach, thawed*
1 *teaspoon celery salt*	½ *pint double cream*
2 *oz uncooked long-grained rice*	*pepper and salt to taste*

Put water, butter, carrots, potatoes, celery salt and $\frac{1}{2}$ teaspoon salt in a large saucepan and simmer for 15 minutes.
Stir in rice and asparagus, cover and simmer for a further 25 minutes.
Drain spinach thoroughly and add to soup. Cover and simmer for five minutes. Stir in 2 teaspoons salt and the cream. Heat but do not boil.
Serves 8.

CHICKEN MARYLAND WITH SWEETCORN FRITTERS

Diane Parker fell in love with this dish when she first went to America. This is the recipe she was given over there but there are many variations. It is important that you use a young chicken of $2\frac{1}{2}$ to 3 lb as it should be tender and tasty.

1 *chicken*	*breadcrumbs*
1 *beaten egg*	$\frac{1}{3}$ *cup water*
flour, salt and pepper	*melted butter, cream*

Divide chicken into four joints. Dip joints into seasoned flour then into beaten egg and finally into breadcrumbs.
Put joints, separated, into well buttered baking tin. Bake in a hot oven (425 F, Gas mark 7) for five minutes then baste well with melted butter and return to oven. Add the water, cover, and cook in a moderate oven (350 F, Gas mark 4) for a further 30-45 minutes. Arrange joints on a hot dish and serve with half a pint of cream sauce – a white sauce made from the pan drippings and cream.

CORN FRITTERS

1 *small tin sweet corn*	$\frac{1}{4}$ *teaspoon paprika*
$\frac{1}{2}$ *cup flour*	1 *tablespoon minced*
1 *teaspoon baking powder*	*parsley*
2 *teaspoons salt*	2 *eggs*

Drain corn in colander and put into basin. Stir in flour sifted with paprika, salt and baking powder. Stir well-beaten egg into the mixture. Drop spoonfuls into deep hot fat and fry till golden and crisp. Drain on crumpled kitchen paper.

CREME BRULEE

No doubt about it – this is a tricky one; and even Mr Booth has been heard to complain that (thanks to Bill Warren interrupting him and distracting his attention at a crucial moment) 'My burnt cream has been utterly ruined. . . .' But when it does succeed, this dessert is a triumph. Since it needs to be well chilled before serving anyway, it can be made the day before you need it – so you can get your headaches over the night before that special dinner party.

4 *eggs yolks*	*bay leaf and a pinch of*
4 *oz castor sugar*	*nutmeg*
1 *pint single cream*	

Beat the egg yolks with 2 oz of sugar until they are light and creamy. Now heat the cream with the nutmeg and bay leaf until it is nearly boiling but not quite. Remove the bay leaf and pour the cream gently on to the egg yolks, beating all the time. Transfer this custard mixture to the top of a double boiler (or use a smaller saucepan over a larger one with boiling water in it). Keep stirring until the custard thickens – but don't let it get too hot, or the egg will curdle.

Pour into a shallow ovenproof dish, and stand this dish in your grill pan, packing the spaces between the two with ice cubes. Very lightly, dredge the remaining 2 oz of sugar over the entire surface of the custard to form a thin, even layer, and put it under the grill. When the sugar has melted and browned take it from the heat and let it cool, then put it in the fridge. Ideally, you should have a crisp 'ice-rink' of browned sugar on top and the creamy smooth custard below; but it may take one or two attempts before you get the knack. Even if you're not lucky first time, don't despair – it still tastes delicious!

Mushrooms a la Grecque
Liver & Onion Casserole
Sailor's Duff

MUSHROOMS A LA GRECQUE

An unusual import from overseas, David's friend, Bob Powell, picked up this recipe from a little 'taverna' when he was on a Greek island holiday, some years ago.

½ lb button mushrooms	1 tablespoon olive oil
½ lb tomatoes	1 teaspoon crushed
1 onion, 1 clove garlic	peppercorns
the juice of 1 lemon	a little chopped parsley,
½ cup chicken stock	seasoning

Peel and chop the onions, garlic and tomatoes. Wash the mushrooms, then heat the oil in a thick-bottomed pan and brown the garlic and onions first, then add the tomatoes and stock, and simmer gently for a few minutes. Next add the mushrooms, peppercorns and seasoning, and carry on simmering for another ten minutes. Then stir in the lemon juice, allow to cool, and put into the fridge – this is a recipe that benefits from being made a day in advance, to chill thoroughly – and garnish with the chopped parsley before serving.

LIVER AND ONION CASSEROLE

This was a favourite dish of Meg's when dining in a little Italian restaurant. She decided to experiment at home and came up with this version. Perhaps not so traditional but certainly just as tasty. It is a cheap dish for these days as the liver need not be calf's. Gentle cooking in a casserole tends to make even the cheaper varieties quite tender.

1 medium slice of liver per person (or two small)	2 large onions
	a sprinkling of mixed herbs
2 slices streaky bacon per person	and Italian seasoning
	salt and pepper to taste

Slice the onions into casserole dish. Lightly flour the liver slices and lay on top. Cut the rind off the bacon and chop into thin strips. (Scissors are best for this.) Add the seasoning. Cover with meat stock or water with two meat cubes and cook in medium oven (375 F, Gas mark 5) for 45 minutes. Stir once or twice and if necessary thicken the gravy 10 minutes before serving.

SAILOR'S DUFF

It's a few years ago now, but at one time Meg's brother Andy served in the Royal Navy, and even after he left the sea and set up his travel agency, he still kept many souvenirs of his service career. This recipe is one of them!

2 *tablespoons butter*	1½ *cups flour*
2 *tablespoons sugar*	¼ *cup boiling water*
½ *cup molasses*	
¼ *teaspoon salt*	**Yellow sauce:**
1 *beaten egg*	2 *egg yolks*
1 *teaspoon baking soda*	1 *cup sugar*
(*dissolved in the hot*	½ *cup cream*
water)	1 *teaspoon vanilla*

Cream butter and sugar, add all other ingredients, boiling water last. Steam for 1½ hours in pudding mould. Serve hot with yellow sauce, made as follows:

Beat the two egg yolks. Add sugar gradually. Set aside until ready to serve pudding then fold in the cream, whipped and flavoured with vanilla. Do not beat this mixture.

Oeufs Mimosa
Crossroads Special Fish Pie
Banana Meringue

OEUFS MIMOSA

Anthony Mortimer found this recipe once during a 'lost weekend' in Monte Carlo (and the less said about that, the better!) It takes its name from the flowers of the mimosa trees, in full bright bloom along the Mediterranean coast even in greyest February and March. . . . And it will brighten up your dinner-party just as effectively.

4 hard-boiled eggs
4 teaspoons mayonnaise
1 teaspoon lemon juice

chopped lettuce, chopped parsley, salt and pepper

Cut the eggs in half longways, scoop out the yolks, then arrange the white halves in pairs on beds of chopped lettuce, flat side up. Now put the four yolks into a bowl and pound them into a paste with the mayonnaise, lemon juice, salt and pepper. Roll the mixture between your finger-tips to make small pellets, each about the size of a pea (and resembling the fluffy flowers of the mimosa). Sprinkle chopped parsley over the halved whites of eggs, then fill each one with a spoonful of the yellow 'flowers'.

CROSSROADS SPECIAL FISH PIE

2 lbs smoked haddock fillet
4 hardboiled eggs
4 tomatoes
1 pint frozen shrimps or prawns (optional)
salt and pepper to taste
breadcrumbs

Cheese sauce
1 pint milk
$\frac{1}{4}$ lb grated cheddar
1 dessert spoonful tomato puree (tomato ketchup will do but remember it has a stronger taste, so perhaps use a little less)
$1\frac{1}{2}$ teaspoons cornflour
2 oz margarine

Bring haddock gently to the boil and simmer for 4-5 minutes. Remove skin and any stray bones and flake into a greased pie dish. Add hardboiled eggs and, if feeling particularly extravagant, the shrimps or prawns are an added luxury. It is wise not to add too much salt at this stage because smoked haddock can sometimes be very salty itself.

Make a thin cheese sauce. Should it thicken too much add a little more milk, stirring all the time so that it does not become lumpy. Pour the cheese sauce over the fish and mix well. Cover with breadcrumbs, decorate with quartered tomatoes and cook in medium oven (400 F, Gas mark 6) for 30 minutes. If the top has not browned, pop under the grill for a few minutes.

BANANA MERINGUE

This is an American favourite introduced to the Crossroads kitchen by Louise Borelli.

2 *level tablespoons custard powder*	4 *bananas*
1 *pint of milk*	1 *level tablespoon jam*
3 *level tablespoons granulated sugar*	2 *level tablespoons castor sugar*
	1 *egg*

Blend the custard powder with 3 to 4 tablespoons of milk. Bring the rest of the milk just to boiling point with the granulated sugar. Stir custard paste again then pour the milk, while still on the boil, into it, stirring all the time. Return to the saucepan and boil for a further minute. Add the yolk of the egg to the custard. Stir in well and cook for two minutes without allowing it to boil. Slice bananas into bottom of fireproof dish, spread with jam and cover with custard. Whisk egg white until stiff, fold in the castor sugar and pile on to custard. Bake in oven at 325 F, Gas mark 3 for about twenty minutes until meringue is set and lightly browned.

Coquilles a la Creme
Savoury Risotto
Apple & Mincemeat Crumble

COQUILLES A LA CREME

This recipe for scallops is very different from the traditional
'St Jacques' method in the half-shell – though some people
say this is the perfect way to serve them. Again, if you'd like
this as a main course, double the quantities.

4 *scallops*	2 *oz butter*
¼ *lb mushrooms*	*salt, pepper*
1 *teaspoon tomato puree*	*lemon juice*
2 *egg yolks*	*a clove of garlic*
2 *tablespoons sherry*	*parsley*
1 *cupful of cream*	*fried bread* (*to garnish*)

Slice the scallops in half, putting aside the red pieces (known
as the 'corals'). Cook the scallops in half the butter, with
salt and pepper, for a few minutes. At the same time, saute
the mushrooms in the rest of the butter, then add these –
together with the sherry and the tomato puree – to the
scallops. Now stir in the cream and beaten egg-yolks; but
take care not to let the mixture boil, or it will curdle. Add the
'corals', together with finely-chopped garlic, chopped
parsley, and a dash of lemon juice, and cook for two more
minutes – then serve with triangles of fried bread.

SAVOURY RISOTTO

Some people say they don't like rice – but then, they may be
people who have never tried any really interesting way of
cooking it. Faye Mansfield once said that, before she came
to work at the Motel as a secretary, she always thought of
rice as the stuff that dreary school puddings were made from.
But the Crossroads chefs taught her that she was mistaken.

33

2 *oz butter*	½ *lb mushrooms*
3 *rashers of bacon*	*powdered saffron (one of*
½ *lb onions*	*those tiny envelopes)*
½ *lb long-grain rice*	2 *tablespoons whipped*
1 *lb tomatoes*	*cream*
1 *glass white wine*	*grated parmesan cheese*
1 *pint chicken stock*	*nutmeg, salt and pepper*

Melt the butter in a sturdy saucepan; fry the chopped bacon rashers in it, then set them aside. Chop the onions and cook these in their turn, until they are soft and golden. Now add the rice and continue cooking until it is transparent, stirring from time to time to make sure it doesn't stick to the pan. Add the chopped and peeled tomatoes, with salt, pepper and a dash of nutmeg – then return the chopped bacon to the mixture. Pour in the wine and the stock, stirring in a little at a time as the rice absorbs the liquid. Last of all, add the peeled, sliced mushrooms and saffron and stir in well. The total cooking time will be about half an hour. Just before serving, stir in the whipped cream, and when you dish up, sprinkle grated cheese over each portion.

APPLE AND MINCEMEAT CRUMBLE

An unusual spring dessert, with distant overtones of Christmas; but you may very well find that you still have some mincemeat that got left over after the festive season. This is an ideal way to use it up.

On the other hand, the 'crumble' is a useful stand-by that will go with any kind of cooked fruit – so you can ring the changes on this recipe over and over again.

For the crumble:	**For the filling:**
8 *oz self-raising flour*	½ *lb mincemeat*
4 *oz butter*	½ *lb peeled, cored and*
6 *oz sugar*	*sliced cooking apples*
grated peel of 1 *lemon*	1 *tablespoon brandy*
	1 *oz sugar*

First make the crumble by rubbing the butter into the flour until it forms small crumbs. Grate the lemon peel and stir this into the mixture, together with the sugar.

Now cook the apple slices – and a tip to remember is that you should always slice across the apple not downwards along the line of the core, otherwise the fruit won't break up and puree smoothly – with just enough water to keep it from burning. When the apple is cooked to a pulp, add the ounce of sugar and re-heat. Mix with the mincemeat and brandy, then pour into an oven-proof dish. Cover with the crumble and bake for 40 minutes in a hot oven (425 F, Gas mark 7).

MENUS FOR SUMMER

Avgolemono
Moussaka
Kisel

AVGOLEMONO

Tina Webb used to have trouble typing this soup on the menus – until she realised that it's got lemon in the ingredients *and* in the spelling. (Avgo-lemon-o!) After that, she never got it wrong again. It comes from Greece originally and may be something of an acquired taste, but if you think you'd enjoy a flavour that combines chicken, egg, and a strong tang of lemon – have a go.

1½ pints chicken stock	3 tablespoons of lemon
1½ oz rice	juice
2 egg yolks	salt and pepper

Bring the chicken stock to the boil, add the rice, and stir it with a wooden spoon, to make sure it doesn't stick to the saucepan. Simmer gently until the rice softens – probably about ten minutes.

Meanwhile, combine the egg yolks, salt, pepper and lemon juice in a bowl, whisking them up together. When the rice is ready, add a ladleful of hot soup to the mixture in the bowl and stir it in well. Continue a spoonful at a time, until about a quarter of the soup has gone in – then pour the contents of the bowl back into the saucepan, still stirring, and heat it through very carefully. Don't let it boil, whatever you do, or the mixture will curdle and you'll finish up with scrambled egg in chicken soup!

MOUSSAKA

After his trip to the near-East with Angela Kelly, David Hunter came back and gave it as his considered opinion that moussaka was really the Greek version of shepherds pie. Certainly both dishes have a basis of minced cooked meat, and are therefore excellent ways of using up leftovers. . . . But perhaps the resemblance really begins and ends there. Moussaka isn't simple to make; it requires time and trouble. But as anyone who ever tasted it will agree – it's very well worth it.

1 *oz butter*	¼ *pint water*
2 *onions*	2 *aubergines*
1 *clove garlic*	2 *tablespoons cooking oil*
1 *lb minced cooked meat*	2 *oz grated cheese*
1 *lb tomatoes*	
3 *tablespoons tomato puree*	**For the white sauce:**
½ *teaspoon nutmeg*	1½ *oz butter*
1 *glass red wine*	3 *oz flour*
1 *tablespoon chopped*	1 *pint milk*
parsley	2 *eggs, salt and pepper*

First of all, the meat; use the minced remains of your Sunday joint – lamb or beef are both equally good. Using a heavy saucepan, fry the chopped onions in the butter until they are golden, then add the crushed garlic and the mince, and fry for five more minutes. Now skin the tomatoes and add these, together with the tomato puree, nutmeg, wine and most of the parsley – just keeping a little back for the final garnish. Pour in the water and let the whole thing simmer for half an hour.

During this time, you can make the white sauce; melt the butter and stir in the flour, then add the milk, a little at a time, stirring continuously until it boils and thickens. Remove from the heat, add salt and pepper; allow to cool slightly, then beat in the eggs.

Slice the aubergines and fry in cooking oil until they are soft. Finally, take an oven dish and put in a layer of aubergines, then a layer of the mince mixture, continuing alternately until they are both used up. Then pour the white sauce over the top, sprinkle with grated cheese, and cook in a moderate oven (350 F, Gas mark 4) for three-quarters of an hour. If it's still not brown enough, finish it off under the grill, and serve with a sprinkling of parsley.

KISEL
Nick Van Doren had trained in hotel management in Switzerland before he came to Crossroads. To the Motel he brought up-to-date efficiency and this simple but exquisite recipe from a restaurant in Geneva.

About 1 lb blackcurrants,   *2-3 tablespoons golden syrup*
raspberries or loganberries   *1 tablespoon cornflour*
1 teacup water

Simmer fruit and water and syrup until soft. Rub through sieve and make up to one pint (if necessary) with a little more water. Blend with cornflour and simmer until smooth for about three minutes. Pour into individual cups and serve with cream or ice cream.

Gazpacho
Paella
Strawberry Cheesecake

GAZPACHO
Another cold soup for a hot day – but with a difference, because of the garnish which you serve separately, on the side. When faced with this array of diced vegetables for the first time, Jim Baines commented suspiciously: 'That 'en't a soup – more like a game of ludo!'

1 *lb tomatoes*   2 *tablespoons of lemon juice*
1 *cucumber*   2 *tablespoons of olive oil*
1 *green pepper*   2 *slices of stale bread*
1 *onion*   *oil for deep frying*
2 *cloves of garlic*   *seasoning*
¼ *pint of water*

Skin and chop up the tomatoes, cucumber, onion; de-seed and chop the green pepper. Now reserve a tablespoonful of each of these for the garnish. Put all the rest, together with *one* crushed clove of garlic, into the blender and liquidise, then combine with the lemon juice, olive oil and water and blend again. Put in the fridge to chill.

Now make garlic croutons, by cutting up the bread into $\frac{1}{4}''$ cubes and deep-frying them in oil that has had the second clove of garlic crushed up in it. When the bread is nice and brown, take it out and drain it. Serve the croutons in a small side dish, along with tiny dishes of the chopped vegetables you reserved earlier; and let your guests enjoy themselves as they pick and choose among these garnishes to decorate the ice-cold soup.

PAELLA

It was probably the very first day that Carlos Rafael turned up for work as chef that he turned to Meg and enquired why 'paella' wasn't on the menu. You wouldn't, he suggested, draw up a menu which didn't include meat – or fish – or rice. So a paella, being all these and more besides, was an essential in every right-minded restaurant.

Meg argued for a while that Midlands diners didn't expect to find such an unusual dish on the bill-of-fare – but finally Carlos talked her to a standstill, and she gave in. Since then, paellas have been in continuous demand, and Meg has to admit that Carlos was undoubtedly right.

$\frac{1}{2}$ *lb long grain rice*
3 *tablespoons cooking oil*
4 *oz peeled prawns*
1 *large onion (chopped)*
2 *tablespoons green peas*
1 *rasher of bacon (chopped)*
4 *slices garlic sausage (chopped)*

1 *green pepper (sliced into matchsticks)*
1 *cupful of diced, cooked chicken*
4 *tomatoes (peeled and chopped)*
$1\frac{1}{2}$ *pints water*
saffron (one envelope)
salt and pepper

40

– and (an optional extra) 6 mussels, still in their shells

If you have a frying pan deep enough to take all these ingredients (including the 1½ pints of water) all well and good – otherwise you must use a heavy saucepan.

Start by warming the oil in the pan, and then sprinkle the rice in evenly over the bottom, and cook for two minutes. Now remove from the heat and pour in the water, then add all the other ingredients (except the mussels). Return to the stove and bring to the boil, stirring all the time. Now reduce the heat and simmer very gently for about twenty minutes, or until all the liquid has been absorbed.

If you are including mussels (and quite frankly they're added more for the look of the thing than anything else) you must cook these separately in boiling water until the shells open; poach them for a few minutes and then keep them on one side and add them to the paella, in their open shells, at the last moment before serving.

STRAWBERRY CHEESECAKE

Glenda Brownlow, who has a teenage terror of putting on weight, always begs Jane Smith not to tell her when this particular sweet is on the menu. 'I can't resist it if I know it's there,' she explains, 'so it's far better for me not to know.'

1 *sponge flan base (you could make your own, but to save time you can always buy one ready-made)*	1 *carton strawberry yoghurt*
	4 *oz cream cheese*
	2 *oz castor sugar*
1 *carton double cream*	1 *punnet strawberries*

Whip the cream, and fold in the yoghurt; then blend in with the cream cheese and sugar. Wash, hull and halve the strawberries; place about half of them on the flan base, then smooth the cream mixture over the top, smoothing with a spatula or broad-bladed knife. Arrange the remaining strawberries in a pattern around the top, and chill in the fridge.

41

Stuffed Courgettes
Mackerel – or Herrings – in Mustard
Gooseberry Fool

STUFFED COURGETTES

Miss Tatum's tastes in food are very definitely English but when Carney drops round with a few courgettes, this is how she cooks them. (As a first course, reduce the quantities by half.)

12 *good sized courgettes*   1 *large onion finely*
    (*about six inches long*)   *chopped*
¾ *lb cold cooked lamb*   1 *good pinch cinnamon*
3-4 *tablespoons long-*   *a little gravy to moisten*
    grained rice   2 *eggs*
3 *tablespoons finely*   *pepper and salt*
    chopped parsley

Trim ends of courgettes, cut in half, scoop out seeds and most of pulp with a teaspoon. Sprinkle insides with a little salt and leave upside down to drain. Mix all ingredients together in a bowl and bind with the eggs. Stuff half the courgettes with the mixture and cover with the remaining halves. Put them in a wide shallow casserole with a little water, cover and cook in a slow oven (300 F, Gas mark 1-2) for one hour or until rice is tender.

Tomato sauce

Drain two 14 oz tins of tomatoes, chop coarsely and add one onion, two cloves of garlic and 2 sprigs of parsley all finely chopped, a good pinch of oregano and half a cup of olive oil. Mix well and simmer in uncovered pan for 50 minutes. Pour over courgettes before serving.

MACKEREL – OR HERRINGS – IN MUSTARD

Being a long way from the sea, the Crossroads Motel usually gets its fish from the deep white freezer rather than the deep blue sea – you're lucky if you live near enough to the coast to buy your fish direct from the morning's catch with the mackerel tails still sticking up like the sails of a yacht, when you pop them into the pan. There's no doubt that the fresher the fish, the better the flavour. But if it has to come from the depths of the fridge, then it's up to you to give the flavour that extra zing. . . . Something like this.

4 *mackerel – or* 4 *herrings*   *chopped parsley and lemon*
French mustard   *juice*
cooking oil or butter as
    required

First the herrings: the best way to deal with them is to take off their heads and split them down the middle, removing all the bones. Then spread the inside of each herring generously with mustard; put the fish back into shape, brush with oil or melted butter, and bake for half an hour (at 350 F, Gas mark 4). Give them a squeeze of lemon juice and a garnishing of parsley, and serve.

As for the mackerel – cut diagonal slashes along both sides of each fish, and fill these with dollops of mustard; then put them under the grill until they are done. Meanwhile, take one or two more teaspoons of mustard and blend it into 2 oz butter, beaten up with the parsley and lemon juice; make up this mustard-butter into little individual pats, and serve one on top of each fish, to melt gently as you dish up.

GOOSEBERRY FOOL

The gooseberry is a typically English fruit and it was first developed in the early nineteenth century by workers in the Midlands who raised seedlings for competitions. In this menu – and in the following one – we show you how it is presented by Crossroads Motel cooks in the late twentieth century in the Midlands!

1 *lb young, green*   *sugar*
    gooseberries   ½ *pint double (whipping)*
2 *oz butter*   *cream*

Top and tail the gooseberries. Melt butter in a large saucepan, add the gooseberries and cook gently for about 5 minutes with the pan covered. When fruit is yellow and softened, remove from the heat and crush the fruit with a fork. They should be made into more of a mash than the puree a liquidiser would produce. Add sugar to taste. Whip the cream until firm then fold in the fruit when it is cold. Add more sugar if necessary and serve, with Langue du Chat sponge fingers or Nice biscuits.

A cheap and emergency substitute for the cream is to make a thick custard and then whip it with the fruit and chill. Tinned gooseberries may also be used.

Serves 6.

Salad Nicoise
Chicken in Lemon Sauce
Gooseberry & Marshmallow Pie

SALAD NICOISE

Probably there will never be one hard-and-fast recipe for Salade Nicoise. After all, the name simply means that it's a summer dish which appeals to the tastes of the inhabitants of Nice – and since Nice has more than 300,000 inhabitants, that must cover a fairly wide range. However, this is the version that is served at Crossroads, but you're at liberty to add or subtract ingredients to suit yourself.

3 tomatoes, cut into quarters	4 anchovy fillets
½ a small onion, sliced into rings	1 hardboiled egg, cut in four longways
1 small green pepper, seeded and then shredded into matchsticks	5 black olives
	1 small tin of tuna fish, broken up into flakes
a handful of radishes	3 tablespoonsful of cooked, sliced green beans
2 stalks of celery, chopped up small	

Mix all the ingredients *except* the anchovies, egg and olives, into a salad bowl. Now make a vinaigrette dressing from:

1 *tablespoon wine vinegar*   1 *crushed clove of garlic;*
2 *tablespoons of olive oil*   ½ *teaspoon sugar*
a pinch of dry mustard;
   salt and black pepper

Whip the dressing up with a fork; or put it in a screwtop jar and shake it enthusiastically. Then pour over the salad and stir it about until it's thoroughly mixed up. Finally decorate the top with a pattern of the egg, olives and anchovies.

CHICKEN IN LEMON SAUCE

A delicious dish for a heatwave; substantial without being heavy, and with a refreshing tang of lemon in the white sauce that gives the chicken a brand-new personality. Meg herself often makes this dish for small family parties at home, on long summer evenings – and it's always a big success.

4 *chicken joints*   1 *tablespoon flour*
4 *rashers bacon*   ½ *pint milk*
1 *bay leaf*   *a pinch of grated nutmeg*
1 *large lemon*   *a carton of soured cream*
2 *oz butter*

Grease an oven dish with a little butter (or use up old butter-papers in this way) and then line the bottom with the four rashers. Arrange the chicken joints on top, together with the bay leaf. Season with salt and pepper and nutmeg. Cut the lemon in half and extract the juice from one half; pour this over the chicken, then add ½ gill of cold water (but not directly on the chicken). Put on the lid and cook in a medium oven (375 F, Gas mark 5) for about an hour and a half. Now transfer the chicken pieces to a serving dish. Take the bacon, and cut off the rinds, then chop the rashers up

45

very finely and sprinkle the result over the chicken. Put this dish aside to keep hot while you make the sauce.

Melt the butter, add the flour, stirring well till it is mixed in. Add the milk a little at a time, and keep on stirring until it is smooth. Bring to the boil, then turn out the heat and stir in the sour cream and the juice from the second half of the lemon. Add salt and pepper and test for flavour; if you like even more of a lemony taste, add some extra lemon juice. Then pour the sauce over the chicken in its serving dish, and bring to the table.

GOOSEBERRY AND MARSHMALLOW PIE

6-8 *oz short crust pastry* 2½ *tablespoons sugar*
1 *lb gooseberries* 1 *tablespoon cornflour*
8 *marshmallows*

Line a 7-8″ pie plate with the pastry, leaving some over for latticework decoration. Stew the gooseberries with a little water and when cooked, sieve them and make a puree by adding up to ⅔ pint water. Mix the cornflour and sugar smoothly with a little of the puree. Heat the remaining puree, adding the cornflour mixture and stirring constantly until boiling. Allow to simmer for one minute. Add a drop or two of green colouring. Pour into pie plate. Roll out remaining pastry into strips. Twist these and arrange in lattice pattern across pie.

Bake for 35 minutes at 400 F, Gas mark 6. Put a marshmallow in each latticework space and cook for a few minutes to brown marshmallows.

Sardines
Veal, Ham & Egg Pie
Summer Pudding

SARDINES

Sardines are very delicate fish and are at their best when freshly caught. However, it is now possible to buy them individually quick-frozen and there is great demand for them when they are on the menu at Crossroads. Bernard Booth serves them in two ways – grilled as a starter or 'au plat' as a fish course.

Grilled Sardines

Allow 4 sardines per person – they are very rich! Slit the belly of the sardine and remove the insides. Wash and wipe the fish with a cloth to remove the loose scales. Dry. Brush lightly with olive oil. Season with salt and pepper. Cook under a grill at not too great a heat. Garnish with sprigs of parsley and lemon slices and serve with brown bread and butter.

Sardines au plat

Put the sardines, seasoned with salt, on a fireproof dish which has been buttered and sprinkled with chopped shallots. Pour over a small glass of dry white wine and the juice of half a lemon. Dot with butter and cook in a fairly hot oven for about 10 minutes. Sprinkle with chopped parsley and serve.

VEAL, HAM AND EGG PIE

Few dishes could be more typically English than this one and, although Shughie McFee swears that his Scottish Game Pie is far superior, the Crossroads veal, ham and egg pie which he makes has won the praise of all who have tasted it. First you will need a hinged pie mould which you can buy from most kitchen shops and for the pastry you must make hot water crust. Here is our recipe.

| 8 *fluid oz water* | 1 *lb plain flour* |
| 6 *oz lard* | ½ *teaspoon salt* |

Bring water and lard to the boil then tip it quickly into the sifted flour and salt and mix it together rapidly with an electric mixer or wooden spoon. As soon as it is cool enough to handle, put just over ⅔ of the dough into the well greased mould and quickly push it up the sides of the mould so that it is completely covered, sides and base, to an even thickness of about quarter of an inch, making sure there are no splits or cracks in it. Roll the remaining dough out to the same thickness to make the lid of the pie.

The fillings:

1½ *lb pie veal*	*grated rind of half a lemon*
¾ *lb uncooked ham,*	1 *tablespoon chopped*
gammon or unsmoked	*parsley*
bacon	1 *teaspoon dried thyme*
salt and pepper	3 *eggs, hardboiled and*
	shelled

Dice veal and ham into ¼″ pieces (don't mince), add seasonings and mix well. Put half into the pie mould, arrange the eggs in a line along it. Cover with remaining meat mixture. Fix lid on pie with beaten egg. Crimp the edges. Cut hole in pie top to allow steam to escape. Decorate with pastry flowers and leaves from trimmings and glaze with the rest of the beaten egg to which a little salt has been added.

Put into oven at 400 F, Gas mark 6 for ½ hour to set the crust then lower heat to 325 F, Gas mark 3 for two hours to cook the meat. Cover pie lid with paper if it appears to brown too quickly. Remove from oven, take it carefully out of mould and brush sides with beaten egg and return to oven for 10 minutes. When cold, fill through hole with jellied stock made by boiling bones from the meat, a pig's trotter, a sliced carrot, an onion, bouquet garni and pepper for 3-4 hours and reduced from about four pints to half a pint. .

SUMMER PUDDING

The soft fruit season is short, though it can be lengthened by
judicious freezing; and we are not all in the position of
owning a fruit-and-vegetable stall like Roy and Sheila
Mollison. But we can borrow Sheila's recipe for using soft
fruit when it is at its best and cheapest. As you see, it is made
overnight; a big help for Sheila, who has it waiting in the
fridge when she gets home from work next day ... all ready
for Roy and little Susan.

  1 *lb redcurrants*
  1 *lb raspberries*
  ¾ *lb granulated sugar*

  1 *small white loaf (slightly
    stale)*

Wash, string and top-and-tail the currants, and wash the
raspberries, then put them into a saucepan with the sugar
and cook over a low heat for 20 minutes. Stir to prevent burning until the juice begins to run, then cover. Remove all the
crusts from the loaf and cut the bread into fairly thin slices.
Line a pudding basin with slices of bread. When the fruit is
cooked, pour some into the bowl and cover with more slices
of bread. Tip in the rest of the fruit and top with a final layer
of bread, folding over the side slices if the fruit doesn't reach
the top. Put a plate on top of the pudding, and weight it
with something heavy. Keep it overnight in the fridge and
serve next day – preferably with whipped cream. (By the way,
this pudding can also be made with blackcurrants, or a
mixture of apples and blackberries.)

Real Tomato Soup
Lobster Salad
Water Melon Flambe

REAL TOMATO SOUP

Sandy always says that, though he prefers some tinned foods
to the other kind (like tinned salmon being really tastier than

fresh salmon, only nobody ever dares to admit it), this is one case where the reverse is true. Once you've tried *real* tomato soup, you'll never want to go back to the kind that comes in cans.

2 *lb ripe tomatoes*	*salt, pepper, a pinch of*
2 *onions*	*mixed herbs, and a pinch*
1 *clove garlic*	*of sugar*
2 *potatoes*	¼ *pint single cream*
¾ *pint chicken stock*	

Peel and chop the tomatoes, onions, garlic and potatoes, then pop them into a saucepan with the chicken stock, seasoning and herbs, and simmer for 25 minutes. Now *either* pass the mixture through a sieve, *or* blend in a liquidiser – then reheat if necessary, but don't let it boil. Before serving, stir in a generous spoonful of cream for each guest.

LOBSTER SALAD
To be strictly honest, this should be called 'Lobster Salad plus . . .' since it uses other fishy ingredients as well. Our recipe is built on the assumption that you can get hold of a 2 lb lobster – but if yours weighs less, just increase the amount of other fish accordingly.

2 *lb boiled lobster*	¼ *lb peas*
½ *lb prawns or scampi*	2 *hardboiled eggs*
½ *lb any white fish*	½ *pint of home-made*
1 *lb new potatoes*	*mayonnaise*
½ *lb french beans*	*a handful of olives, and*
¼ *lb diced carrots*	*watercress for garnish*

Shell the lobster carefully; slice up the body, reserve the flesh from the claws and save it for the garnish, along with half a dozen prawns still in their shells. Peel the rest, and mix with the remainder of the lobster meat from the legs etc. Cook the white fish in boiling water until it is firm; drain, remove all the skin and bones, and flake. Add to the mixed shellfish. Now boil the potatoes, beans, carrots and peas – but make sure they are not overcooked; the vegetables should be crisp, not mushy. Drain them and leave to cool. Slice the boiled potatoes thinly, and mix all these vegetables into the prepared mayonnaise. Heap the mixed fish on to a large serving-dish, and surround with a ring of the vegetable mayonnaise; garnishing at intervals with slices of hard-boiled egg, olives, and small sprigs of watercress. Finally decorate with the pink flesh from the lobster claws, and the unshelled prawns.

WATERMELON FLAMBE

A party dish to serve 20 people. Ex-barman, Jeff Gilbert, tasted this superb sweet at a barbecue party he went to, last summer. It makes a spectacular finale to an open-air meal or that extra special occasion.

1 *big, ripe water melon*	$\frac{1}{2}$ *lb grated coconut*
fresh fruit as available	$\frac{1}{2}$ *lb pineapple preserve*
juice of one or two lemons	$\frac{1}{2}$ *lb apricot jam*
1 *large (15 oz) tin pineapple*	1 *cup of rum*
chunks	

Cut a slab lengthways in a zig-zag pattern from the side of the water melon. Scoop out the melon into balls. Combine these with balls from a honeydew or cantaloupe melon, grapes, peaches, cherries, or whatever fresh fruit is available. Sprinkle thoroughly with lemon juice to prevent discolouration and chill in a large bowl together with the melon shell. When ready for serving, heat in a pan the pineapple chunks, the coconut and the preserves. Put the chilled fruit in the water melon shell and pour over it the heated mixture. Sprinkle over the cup of well warmed rum and set alight.

Crab en Cocotte
Blanquette de Veau
Fresh Strawberry Souffle

CRAB EN COCOTTE

An unusual hot, rich beginning to a meal – but be warned! The Crossroads restaurant once served it to an over-ambitious diner who enjoyed it so much that he ordered a second helping . . . then complained bitterly when he was attacked by indigestion later.

1 *dressed crab*	1 *teaspoon dry mustard;*
4 *slices of white bread*	*salt and black pepper*
without crusts	*Worcester sauce*
1 *small carton of double*	*breadcrumbs, and melted*
cream	*butter*

Turn the crabmeat into a mixing bowl, being careful to make sure that no tiny scraps of shell creep in by mistake (Jill Harvey says that biting on an unexpected fragment of shell is one of life's little miseries – like stepping on a step that isn't there.) Cut the bread up into small cubes; then stir the mustard, salt, pepper and a dash of Worcester sauce (to taste) into the cream. Pour all this over the bread, and then fold the crabmeat in.

Transfer the mixture to four individual ovenproof dishes (known technically as 'cocottes' or in English 'ramekins'), sprinkle the tops with breadcrumbs and dribble a little melted butter over each one. Then bake for five to ten minutes in a pre-heated slow oven (350 F, Gas mark 4). They should be golden-brown on top, and if they're not quite sunburnt enough at the end of the cooking-time, you can pop them under the grill for a moment to finish them off.

BLANQUETTE DE VEAU

Whenever she is in Paris, Rosemary Hunter (now living in Switzerland) visits her favourite little bistro where 'le patron' prepares her this favourite dish.

$1\frac{1}{2}$ lb fillet of veal cut into	1 small bay leaf
thinnish slices	1 clove
$1\frac{1}{2}$ oz butter	1 lb small potatoes
$\frac{1}{3}$ pint stock	flour, salt, pepper

Melt fat in frying pan. Dip pieces of veal into seasoned flour and fry until brown all over. Put into stewpan. Add stock, bay leaf and clove and arrange peeled potatoes around. Cover and simmer for an hour and a half. Remove potatoes to one hot dish and veal to another. Add a little water or stock to the gravy in the stewpan, bring to the boil, stir well then pour through strainer over the veal.

FRESH STRAWBERRY SOUFFLE

This is a great favourite with all the guests during the height of summer. It was also one of the dishes used to tempt Sandy's appetite after his accident. He never could resist strawberries in any shape or form. Our chef's tip to make this an extra special dessert: place a mug or jar, lightly oiled on the outside with olive oil, in the centre of the mixture when leaving it to set. Remove this and fill the hole with real strawberries topped with ice cream or whipped cream – delicious! This recipe does equally well with loganberries or raspberries.

$\frac{1}{4}$ pt cream (or evaporated	$\frac{1}{2}$ teacup water
milk)	2 eggs
$\frac{1}{4}$ pt thick strawberry puree	2 oz sugar
(made by rubbing them	few drops of lemon juice
through a sieve)	few drops vanilla essence
$1\frac{1}{4}$ teaspoons powdered	cream and whole
gelatine	strawberries to decorate

Whip the cream or evaporated milk. Dissolve the gelatine in the water and add to the strawberry puree. Whisk this mixture into the cream. It is important to be quick and vigorous at this stage to prevent any possibility of the mixture curdling. Separate the yolks from the whites of the eggs, mix the yolks with the sugar, lemon juice and vanilla in a basin over hot water, then beat until thick and creamy. Remove and continue to beat until cold, then stir gently into the strawberry and cream mixture. Whip the egg whites until very stiff and fold into the mixture. Put into a souffle dish and allow to set. Decorate with whipped cream and strawberries.

Salmon Mousse
Lamb Curry
Strawberry Shortcake

SALMON MOUSSE
Here is a favourite recipe for receptions and other such functions at Crossroads. The garnishing of the dish gives one great artistic scope. But don't overdo it and make the mousse look like a vegetable garden!

1 *packet gelatine*	¼ *teaspoon paprika*
2 *tablespoons lemon juice*	½ *teaspoon basil and*
1 *small slice of onion*	*tarragon mixed*
4 *oz boiling water (about*	2 × 7½ *oz tins salmon,*
half a teacupful)	*drained*
4 *oz mayonnaise (about*	⅓ *pint double cream*
half a teacupful)	

Empty the envelope of gelatine into the container of an electric blender. Add the lemon juice, onion and boiling water. Place cover on the container and blend at high speed for 40 seconds. Switch off and add mayonnaise, paprika, basil, tarragon and salmon. Cover and blend briefly. Add the cream, one third at a time, blending for a few seconds after each addition. Blend thirty seconds longer, then pour into ½ pint mould, fish-shaped if you have one. Chill. Unmould when set and garnish with cucumber and lemon slices. Serves 6.

LAMB CURRY

This is one of Dr. Farnham's favourites and is always available in the Cafeteria at Crossroads.

1½ oz cooking fat or margarine

2 lb shoulder or leg of lamb cut into cubes

2-3 medium sized onions, chopped

2 cloves of garlic, crushed

½ teaspoon salt

½ teaspoon ground ginger

¼ teaspoon pepper

¼ teaspoon ground cumin

1-2 tablespoons curry powder

1 teaspoon flour

juice of half a lemon

1 tin condensed beef broth

1 cup water

Heat fat in large frying pan. Add meat, brown it and set aside. Soften onions and garlic in remaining fat. Add flavourings and flour and cook for two minutes stirring constantly to avoid burning.

Return lamb to frying pan, add beef broth and water. Reduce the heat, cover and cook slowly for about 45 minutes, stirring occasionally until meat is tender. Serve with rice and chutney.

STRAWBERRY SHORTCAKE

When the strawberry season first begins, the fresh fruit are so welcome that the Motel usually serves them to guests 'neat' – at least, simply with cream and sugar on the side. But if it's a long season, the chefs like to ring the changes after a while, and this is a very popular way of dealing with strawberries at the peak of the summer.

2 eggs

4 oz butter

4 oz castor sugar

5 oz self-raising flour

1 tablespoon hot water

a pinch of salt

1 lb strawberries

½ pint double cream

Grease two sandwich tins and dust them with a little flour. Sift the rest of the flour with the salt. Cream the butter and sugar thoroughly, then break the eggs into this mixture one at a time, and stir in. Mix thoroughly, adding the hot water at the last moment. Pour the mixture into the sandwich tins and cook in a very moderate oven (350 F, Gas mark 4) for 25 minutes. When the cakes are done, turn out on a wire tray to cool.

Whip the cream, hull, wash and halve the strawberries. Now spread one cake with a layer of half the cream, and add a layer of half the strawberries. Put the other cake on top, repeating the process with two more layers of cream and strawberries; put in the fridge to chill, and serve.

Vichysoisse
Sole with Grapes and Cheese Sauce
Granita

VICHYSOISSE

This can be served hot or cold, but Mr Booth finds that it's most popular as a chilled soup for summertime lunches.

2 *leeks*	½ *pint single cream*
1 *onion*	½ *oz butter*
1 *lb cooked potatoes*	*salt and pepper*
1 *pint chicken stock*	*chopped chives for*
½ *pint milk*	*garnishing*

Wash the leeks and slice them finely; peel and chop the onion. Cook these in butter until they are just 'coloured'; then add the stock, milk and potatoes, and cook for about ten minutes. Now liquidise, season to taste, allow to cool, then add the cream, stirring in well. Chill, sprinkle with chives, and serve.

SOLE WITH GRAPES AND CHEESE SAUCE

Sole is never cheap, and you could try a more economic version of this recipe by using fillets of plaice instead; though

56

of course for high days and holidays, sole is undoubtedly the perfect fish for this luxury dish. When the Motel first opened, Meg remembers that fish on the menu was always something of a gamble, because the Motel was dependent on whatever the Kings Oak fishmonger had in stock. But once the deep freeze came into service, it simply became a question of stockpiling when prices were at their lowest, and – as Jim Baines would say – 'Bob's yer flippin' uncle!'

4 *fillets of sole*	1½ *oz flour*
16 *white grapes*	½ *pint warm milk*
salt and pepper	1 *teacup grated cheese*
	1 *tablespoon cream*

For the cheese sauce:
2 *oz butter*

Make the sauce as described in the recipe for Chicory with Ham (page 103). Meanwhile, wash the fillets and sprinkle with salt and pepper. Wash the grapes, halve them and remove the pips. Put the grapes along each fillet, then roll it up around them, pinning it together with a cocktail stick. Place them in an oven dish, pour the cheese sauce over, and cook for half an hour (350 F, Gas mark 4).

GRANITA
This isn't a coffee ice-cream so much as a coffee sorbet or water-ice. It's crunchy, almost bittersweet in flavour, and appeals to the kind of diners who would never consider ordering a dessert in the ordinary way.

3 *tablespoons instant coffee*	3 *tablespoons sugar*
granules	6 *ice cubes*
½ *pint water*	*whipped cream*

Make up the coffee with the water, instant coffee and sugar, bringing to the boil and simmering for five minutes. Then remove from the heat and stir in the ice cubes until they melt. Now pour into a freezer-box and put into the freezer (if you have one) or the cold-store compartment of your fridge. After about an hour and a half (though it's difficult to be specific about the timing, because it all depends on the temperature of the freezer) the ice should be hardened around the edges but soft in the middle. At this stage, turn it into a bowl and whisk with an electric mixer until it is evenly smooth. Now return to the freezer and freeze until it is almost solid. To serve, spoon it into individual glasses, and top each one with a dollop of whipped cream.

Tabouleh
Baked Mackerel with Gooseberry Sauce
Angel Wine Cake

TABOULEH
Some years ago, after Meg and the Crossroads staff had enjoyed their stay in the Tunisian island of Djerba, they brought back with them the recipes for several traditional Tunisian and Arabic dishes. Tabouleh originated in the Lebanon but is widely used throughout the Arab world. Crossroads gets many visitors from the Middle East and they are always very surprised and pleased to find that their tastes are catered for.

1 *cup of wheatmeal porridge or crushed wheat*	2 *cups chopped tomatoes*
	lemon juice
1 *cup chopped mint*	*oil*
1 *cup chopped parsley*	*salt and pepper*
½ *cup minced onion*	

Soak the wheat in water for 15 minutes and then wring out through a muslin cloth. Stir the onion, tomato, mint and parsley into the wheat and sprinkle with about 3 tablespoons of lemon juice and enough oil to bind the mixture together. Add a very little salt and freshly ground pepper. Serve in individual bowls and instead of spoons use fresh cos lettuce leaves as scoops.

BAKED MACKEREL WITH GOOSEBERRY SAUCE

Tish Hope always claims that gooseberries are an under-rated fruit, with their unique sweet-and-sour taste. (Perhaps it's because Tish has a certain sweet-and-sour quality herself!) Be that as it may – here's a really unusual way of using ripe gooseberries, in a fish recipe with a difference.

4 *mackerels*	½ *oz butter*
¼ *pint gooseberry puree*	½ *oz flour*
¼ *pint milk (previously warmed)*	1 *tablespoonful cream*
	salt and pepper

Wrap up each fish in tin foil like a small parcel; and then bake them in a moderate oven (400 F, Gas mark 6) for fifteen or twenty minutes.

Make up the gooseberry puree by sieving the fruit or using a blender (but of course remembering it won't need additional sweetening). Then prepare a sauce by melting the butter in a thick pan, add the flour, and cook for a minute or two longer; then pour in the warm milk and stir continuously until the mixture thickens, at boiling point. Simmer a few moments longer, then add the cream and remove from the heat. Now mix in the gooseberry puree to complete the sauce. Unpack the fish parcels, and arrange the mackerel on a serving dish, sprinkling with salt and pepper. Serve the gooseberry sauce separately.

ANGEL WINE CAKE

During her term of office as a cook at the Motel, Cynthia Cunningham produced some very luscious and tempting desserts – none more so than this particular recipe, which is rich yet light and a blend of sophistication and simplicity ... all qualities that the Motel came to associate with the lovely lady herself.

2 *eggs*	½ *oz baking powder*
8 *oz castor sugar*	½ *lb strawberries*
½ *lemon*	4 *tablespoons strawberry*
vanilla essence	*jam*
1 *wineglass of white wine*	*whipped cream for*
1 *wineglass of cooking oil*	*decoration*
8 *oz flour*	

Break the eggs into a mixing-bowl and beat with the sugar. Squeeze the lemon and set aside the juice, then grate the rind and add this to the mixture, together with a few drops of vanilla essence. Whisk thoroughly, then add the wine, oil and lemon juice, and continue to beat. Finally add the flour, and carry on beating until it is well-mixed. At the very end, stir in the baking powder. Fill a buttered ring-mould with the mixture (if you have one) or two shallow sandwich tins if you haven't. Bake in the centre of the oven at 400 F, Gas mark 6 for 45 minutes. Let the sponge cool in the tin and don't try to turn it out until it is quite cold.

Now – if it's a ring mould, fill the centre with the washed, hulled and halved strawberries, with the jam stirred in and decorative rosettes of whipped cream over the top. Or if you're using the sandwich tins, make a layer of the same strawberry-and-cream filling between the two halves, and dust the top with icing sugar.

Cold Cucumber & Mint Soup
Crab Bouillabaisse
Makroudhs

COLD CUCUMBER AND MINT SOUP

When Hugh was in the Balkans he discovered that one of their greatest specialities was yoghurt and he particularly enjoyed a cucumber and yoghurt soup called 'tarator'. Shughie McFee produced this soup and challenged Hugh to say that 'that foreign soup' was better. It wasn't and this soup is often on the summer menus at Crossroads.

1 *medium sized cucumber, unpeeled, sliced*
1 *tin chicken consomme*
the same amount of soured cream
$\frac{1}{4}$ *teaspoon ground black pepper*
a handful of fresh mint
salt to taste

Place all the ingredients in a blender and mix until nearly smooth. Chill in cups and serve garnished with finely sliced cucumber peel.

CRAB BOUILLABAISSE

A proper bouillabaisse cannot be made anywhere but on the shores of the Mediterranean as some of the fish that are essential to the dish cannot be found anywhere else. But he was far from the sea when David Hunter was given this dish – Switzerland in fact!

$7\frac{1}{2}$ *oz tin crabmeat*
3 *chopped onions*
3 *tablespoons olive oil*
2 *green peppers cut into thin strips*
2 *potatoes peeled and sliced*
2 *teaspoons salt*
1 *clove garlic, chopped fine*
1 *bay leaf*
3 *tablespoons tomato paste*
1 *pint boiling water*
1 *lb white fish fillets cut into one inch pieces*
chopped parsley
$\frac{1}{2}$ *lb peeled prawns or shrimps*

Saute onions in oil in a large pan until tender but not brown. Add green peppers and potatoes. Cook for five minutes. Add salt, garlic, bay leaf, tomato paste and boiling water. Cover and simmer for twenty minutes. Add fish fillets and cook for ten minutes. Add crabmeat and shrimps and simmer for a further fifteen minutes. Serve in deep bowls garnished with chopped parsley. Hot French bread should accompany this dish.

MAKROUDHS

And here is another of Meg's discoveries – like 'Tabouleh', this is a very different dessert which Meg brought back from Tunisia.

1¼ lb semolina	7 fluid oz of oil
5¼ oz dates	oil for frying
1 large pinch of salt	golden syrup or honey

Place the semolina in a large dish, heat the oil and pour on to semolina, mixing it well with a little warm water, to form a firm but not hard paste. Do not knead it. Divide into two large balls. Flatten the balls with the palm of the hand on a bread board to a thickness of ¼–½". Stone and finely chop the dates and add to mixture. Roll out the pastry and cut into slices ½" wide. Fry in hot oil – 4 or 5 together. Finally dip the makroudhs in the honey or golden syrup, and arrange on a dish for serving.

Real Asparagus Soup
Devilled Lamb Cutlets
Pavlova

REAL ASPARAGUS SOUP

Another home-made vegetable soup – and this one is a real winner. Asparagus equals luxury, without a doubt; and no wonder it's not cheap to buy. But there is a moment, at the beginning of the asparagus season, when you can treat yourself to this delicious extravagance without breaking the bank . . . when the growers thin out their crop, and the greengrocer sells very slim stalks, very reasonably, as 'thinnings'. These are the kind to make into soup.

2 pints chicken stock	1 heaped tablespoon plain
1 lb asparagus thinnings	flour
2 oz butter	bay leaf, salt and pepper to
cream	taste

Cut the green tips off the thinnings and put them aside; chop up the rest of the stalks, and add to the stock, with salt and pepper. Simmer gently for one hour. Now melt the butter in a thick pan, and add the flour gradually, stirring it in as the butter melts. Pour a ladleful of the soup into this, stirring constantly, until you have a smooth sauce, adding more soup as required. Add this sauce in turn to the main pan of soup, as a thickening agent, and stir again. Now blanch the asparagus tips in boiling water for a few minutes, and add them to the soup. Check the seasoning once more, and serve – with a spoonful of cream on top of each bowl.

DEVILLED LAMB CUTLETS

Although this dish includes curry among its ingredients, it doesn't resemble an Eastern curry in any way – and even guests who don't like Indian dishes have been persuaded to try this, with successful results. It's hot and spicy, but surprisingly light – so it makes a wonderful way to tempt a jaded appetite on a warm summer day.

8 *lamb cutlets*	1 *small carton double cream*
1 *tablespoon curry paste*	*salt and pepper*
2 *teaspoons French mustard*	

Trim excess fat from the cutlets; mix the curry paste with mustard, and then stir in the cream carefully, adding salt and pepper. Spread the mixture over the cutlets on both sides, leaving them as long as possible so that the flavour really has time to soak into the meat.

Make a tray of kitchen foil on the wire mesh of your grill pan, and arrange the cutlets on top. Cook under the grill for about five minutes, then turn the cutlets to cook for another five on the other side. Some of the sauce will run off the meat inevitably, so spoon it up and use it as a baste – and when you dish up, scrape up all the left-over sauce from the foil and pour it over . . . it's too good to waste!

PAVLOVA

The first time Sandy tasted this very rich sweet, he enquired how it got its name. Mr Lovejoy informed him that it was named in honour of the world-famous ballerina. Sandy pondered this for a moment then said, 'I bet that must have slowed up her Dying Swan quite a bit.'

3 *egg whites*	*fresh or bottled fruit*
6 *oz castor sugar*	*a carton of double cream*
½ *teaspoon vanilla essence*	

First make a meringue; whisk the egg whites until they are very stiff and stand up in peaks. Add half the sugar and carry on beating for a few more minutes, then fold in the remaining sugar and the vanilla. Line an 8″ sandwich tin with foil, and spoon the mixture on to this, first over the bottom, then letting the meringue build up round the sides until it makes a 'nest' with a hollow in the middle.

Place this in the middle of a very slow oven (250 F, Gas mark ¼) for about 1½ hours, until it is crisp outside but still soft inside. Turn it upside down on to a serving dish and leave to cool, then peel off the foil carefully. As it cools it will shrink; if you're lucky, it will shrink all in one piece, but most likely it will crack here and there. Since it is to be used as the shell for a semi-liquid filling, you will then have to turn it into a glass dish (like a salad bowl) big enough to hold the whole thing – or you'll finish up with the table awash in fruit juice.

Either way, the next stage is to fill the meringue with soft fruit – strawberries, raspberries, or blackcurrants in season – or a mixture of fruit (one of the most successful blends at the Motel is lightly-stewed blackberries in a little syrup, combined with bottled apricots). Finally, whip the cream and pipe it over the top in decorative swirls or rosettes. Chill in the fridge and serve.

ICED CHICKEN CURRY SOUP

When Dr. Hilary Maddox and her flatmate, Eileen Blythe, give an informal supper party for their friends, they often start with this soup. It is another which can be made well in advance.

2 *tins chicken broth with*	1 *teaspoon curry powder*
rice	*Rose's lime marmalade*
an equal quantity of milk	*salt and pepper to taste*

Mix soup, milk and curry powder in a blender. Season. Put a small amount of lime marmalade ($\frac{1}{2}$ teaspoon) in the centre of the cups. Pour soup into cups. Chill well and serve. A quick emergency recipe when friends call unexpectedly can be made by blending two tins of cream of chicken soup, two tins of unsweetened Carnation milk, 2 teaspoons curry powder, salt and pepper to taste. Chill in fridge and serve garnished with parsley or chives.
Serves 6.

SEAFOOD RISOTTO

A different method of cooking rice – and a surprisingly simple one. The ingredients give the dish a tangy, sea-food flavour – but if you prefer, you could use chopped ham, kidney, or chicken livers instead: it's a recipe that adapts itself easily to any variation. In the same way, if you haven't got a ring-mould, use a pudding basin, and when you turn the rice out, make a hollow in the top as a 'nest' for the savoury filling.

$\frac{1}{2}$ *lb long-grain rice*	1 *tin sardines*
1 *onion*	2 *oz prawns and/or pieces*
2 *oz butter*	*of crabmeat*
1 *tin tomato juice*	*pepper*

Wash the rice well and put it in a heavy saucepan, with the lump of butter and the onion, finely chopped. Now pour in tomato juice until the level of liquid covers the rice by about a quarter of an inch. Bring it to the boil once, then turn down to the lowest possible heat: if you have a gas-stove, the flame should be a small blue bead. Cook it at this temperature for 15 minutes, then turn out the heat altogether and let it stand for a further 10 minutes – until all the liquid is absorbed in the rice.

Meanwhile, in a separate saucepan, heat through the chopped sardines, pieces of crab and peeled prawns in a little butter, adding a dash of pepper. Turn the cooked rice into a greased ring-mould, pressing down well and keeping hot; after a few minutes you can turn it out and it will keep its shape. Fill the centre with the savoury fish mixture, and serve.

ICE-CREAM FOR A WEDDING

. . . And that is exactly what it is; a very special ice-cream which was served up, with fresh fruit salad, as the dessert at Meg and Hugh's wedding reception at the Droitwich Hotel. Even at that very happy moment, Meg still made a mental note: this was something to be added to the Crossroads Motel repertoire. So before the happy couple left for their honeymoon, she contrived to wheedle the recipe out of the Droitwich chef!

12 *halves of meringue*
   (bought ready-made, or
   made at home if you
   prefer)
grated rind of 1 lemon

¾ *pint double cream*
4 *pieces of ginger, preserved*
   in syrup
3 *tablespoons kirsch*
2 *tablespoons castor sugar*

Whisk the cream until it is stiff. Chop the ginger finely. Grate the rind of the lemon, then fold the ginger, sugar, lemon rind and kirsch into the cream. Break the meringues up into small pieces and stir these in as well.

Now line a cake-tin with a lightly greased piece of kitchen foil. (All in one piece, so it won't leak.) Spoon in the mixture and pack it down firmly, leaving no air-holes. Cover with another piece of foil and put in the freezer overnight. About a quarter of an hour before you want to serve it, take out the ice-cream by removing the foil lining from the tin – and then serve with an accompanying fruit salad. (Enough for 8 people.

MENUS FOR AUTUMN

Watercress Soup
Beef Chasseur
Apricot Crumble

WATERCRESS SOUP

This soup is equally good served hot or cold – in summer, a well-chilled soup makes a refreshing starter on a hot, sunny day. (Though with our uncertain weather, 'first catch your hot, sunny day' – as Mrs Beeton might have said.)

2 *bunches of watercress*	½ *pint chicken stock*
1 *lb potatoes*	½ *pint milk*
1 *onion*	¼ *pint single cream*
1 *oz butter*	*salt and pepper*

Wash the watercress thoroughly; keep some of the smaller sprigs aside for garnishing. Cut off and throw away the really thick stalks, then chop up all the rest. Peel and chop the potatoes and onion. Melt the butter in a heavy saucepan, and fry the onion gently for a few minutes; then add the potatoes and watercress and carry on frying for another five minutes, stirring well to make sure it doesn't catch. Pour in the stock and milk, add seasoning and bring to the boil – then cover with a lid and leave it to simmer very gently for ¾ hour. Meanwhile, remove all the stalks from the remaining watercress sprigs, just keeping the leaves.

When the soup is cooked, liquidise it (either through a sieve or in the blender) and then let it cool and chill it in fridge if you want to serve it cold. Stir in the cream just before bringing it to the table.

If you prefer it hot, reheat without boiling after it has been liquidised, and then add the cream. In either case, sprinkle the garnish of watercress leaves on the top at the last moment.

BEEF CHASSEUR

'Chasseur' is the French for 'huntsman' – and the theory is that the hungry hunter (not you, David) collected some mushrooms and wild onions on his way home through the wild autumnal woods, together with a small bottle of wine (presumably hunted from some wild autumnal wine-cellar). Like all theories, it doesn't bear close examination – but this recipe for beef, sauteed in a mushroom, wine and onion sauce, will pass any examination with distinction.

1½ lb skirt of beef	1 dessertspoon tomato puree
2 tablespoons cooking oil	1 clove garlic
1 dessertspoon butter	salt, pepper, mixed herbs
1 onion	½ pint beefstock
1 tablespoon flour	½ lb mushrooms
1 glass white wine	

Cut the meat up into bite-sized pieces; chop the onion and crush the garlic with salt. Wash and slice the mushrooms. Put the butter and oil into a thick stewpan, and when they start to bubble, add the meat and cook quickly until it is browned. Remove the meat, and put in the chopped onion. When the onion is soft, add the flour and go on cooking until this too is a good rich brown. Now add the wine, tomato puree, chopped garlic and stock. Stir until it comes to the boil, add mixed herbs and the meat. Reduce the heat, cover the pan and let it simmer for fifty minutes; then add the mushrooms, cook for ten more minutes, and serve.

APRICOT CRUMBLE

Here is a dish which is as English as Amy Turtle! Many other fruits can be used instead – pears (first stewed in a little water), or tinned peaches are particularly good, or blackcurrants when in season, or apple and blackberries.

1 large tin apricots or about two dozen fresh apricots or soaked dried apricots	4 oz soft brown sugar, pale
	1 teaspoon ground ginger
	½ saltspoon baking powder
8 oz plain flour	6 oz butter

Drain apricots well, if tinned. Otherwise pour boiling water over them, leave for a few minutes before peeling and stoning them. Place sliced apricots in greased pie dish and if using fresh apricots, sprinkle with sugar. Cover with crumble mixture made in this way: Mix flour, sugar and baking powder together. Rub in butter until you have a crumb-like mixture. Cover apricots and cook until golden brown at 350 F, Gas mark 4 for about 35 minutes. Serve with double cream.

Scampi in Curry and Cream
Stuffed Marrow
Apple Butterscotch Pie

SCAMPI IN CURRY AND CREAM

An exotic flavour, certainly, but it's not a fierce curry – so don't worry, it's not going to blow the top of your head off.

1 *large onion*	1 *level tablespoon flour*
$\frac{1}{4}$ *pint water*	*juice of half a lemon*
1 *heaped teaspoon tomato puree*	8 *oz scampi (or peeled prawns if they're easier to come by)*
1 *tablespoon chutney*	
1 *tablespoon olive oil*	$\frac{1}{2}$ *oz butter*
1 *level tablespoon curry powder*	3 *tablespoons double cream*

Cut the onion in half: peel and finely chop each half, but keep them separate. You'll need to use the first half now, and save the rest till later. Heat the oil in a thick-bottomed saucepan, and fry the first lot of onion for about five minutes, until it's softened. Stir in the curry powder and carry on frying a little longer, then stir in the flour. Add the water, a little at a time, stirring until the mixture is boiling, then add the tomato puree, chutney and lemon juice. Simmer for five minutes more, then put aside to keep warm.

Wash and dry the scampi (or prawns); heat the butter in a frying-pan and cook the chopped onion that you've had standing by, adding the scampi when the onion is gently frying. Stir the scampi in until it's thoroughly heated, then pour in the sauce and let the whole lot come up to just below boiling-point. Then stir in the cream, and serve.

STUFFED MARROW

Marrows are not strong in flavour so it is important to make a really savoury stuffing. Here is how the chefs deal with it at Crossroads.

1 *medium marrow*	1 *level teaspoon tomato*
1 *tablespoon olive oil*	*puree*
1 *medium to large onion,*	1 *teaspoon mixed herbs*
chopped	1 *teaspoon pepper and salt*
1 *lb raw minced beef*	12 *Spanish stuffed olives,*
2 *oz mushrooms, chopped*	*sliced*
1 *oz breadcrumbs* (*white*)	

Take a slice off the top of the marrow and remove seeds with a spoon. Put the olive oil into a frying pan, add the onion and fry until soft. Add the minced beef and cook for a further five minutes. Stir in all the other ingredients then put them into the hollowed-out marrow. Replace the top and completely seal the marrow in foil. Place in baking dish and cook for 1½ hours at 375 F, Gas mark 5.

APPLE BUTTERSCOTCH PIE

What would we do without the apple? We drink its juice in various forms from a non-alcoholic health drink to a very strong spirit. We can start a meal with iced, curried apple soup, continue with Pork Chops Normandes (see the recipe on page 89) and finish with a variety of apple fritters, pies or puddings. (Incidentally, fried apple slices are a perfect complement to bacon as a breakfast dish.)

8 oz flaky pastry
1½ oz butter
1½ lb apples

3 oz demerara sugar
water

Simmer the apples (peeled, cored and sliced) with the butter, sugar and a very little water, until you have a fairly thick puree. Roll out pastry and use half to cover a 7″ pie plate thinly. Fill with apple and cover with remaining pastry. Knock up edges, decorate, cut slit in middle, brush with milk and bake in the centre of a hot oven (425 F, Gas mark 7) for twenty minutes. Then lower heat to 375 F, Gas mark 5 for a further 20 minutes until the pastry is golden in colour and cooked.

Mexican Scallops
Chicken Hunter Style
Paradise Cake

MEXICAN SCALLOPS
Here is another legacy of Carlos's regime in the Crossroads kitchen.

8 scallops
the juice of two lemons
½ lb tomatoes
1 small green pepper
4 tablespoons olive oil
2 tablespoons white wine
   vinegar

3 tablespoons chopped
   parsley
½ teaspoon chopped oregano
salt and black pepper
1 avocado pear
about 6 pimento stuffed
   olives

Cut the well cleaned scallops into two or three slices, leaving the orange corals whole. Put all these into a bowl, cover with lemon juice and leave to marinate for at least 4 hours, turning several times. Remove seeds and pith from pepper and cut into small dice. Peel and seed tomatoes and cut into small dice. Mix olive oil and vinegar thoroughly then add with peppers, tomatoes and seasoning to the scallops. Stir all together carefully but well. Peel avocado and cut into small dice. Add this to the bowl, ensuring that each piece is covered with dressing to avoid discolouring. Add sliced stuffed olives. Transfer to serving dish and serve well chilled.

CHICKEN HUNTER STYLE

You may be disappointed to discover that, just as the 'Beef Chasseur' recipe really means beef stewed in the way a huntsman might find easiest (with white wine, mushrooms and onion), so this is a way of preparing chicken with a similar sauce. And yet, after all, perhaps it *has* got something to do with our Mr Hunter – since this happens to be one of David's favourite recipes.

4 *chicken joints*
flour, salt and pepper
3 *oz butter*
1 *onion*
1 *large tin of tomatoes*

$\frac{1}{4}$ *pint white wine*
1 *bay leaf*
$\frac{1}{4}$ *lb button mushrooms*
chopped parsley

Toss the chicken joints in seasoned flour, and then brown them in the melted butter (saving about half an ounce of the butter until later). Place the joints in a casserole, then fry the chopped onion until it is golden. Transfer the onion to the casserole, together with the tomatoes (also the liquid they came in) and wine, with the seasoning and bay leaf. Put on the lid and cook in a moderate oven (350 F, Gas mark 4) for 1½ hours. At the end of this time, sautee the mushrooms in the remaining butter, and add them to the casserole; cook for five more minutes, then sprinkle with chopped parsley and serve.

PARADISE CAKE

When Hugh first went out to Australia on business he was introduced to this gorgeous combination of cream, cake and

74

fresh fruit which will never be found in any weight watchers cookery book!

For cake:
5 *tablespoons corn oil*
5 *tablespoons water*
2 *eggs*
5 *oz plain flour*
1 *saltspoon salt*
1 *tablespoon cornflour*
6 *oz castor sugar*
1 *heaped teaspoon baking*
   powder

juice of ½ a large orange
1 *oz sugar*
1 *egg yolk*
½ *oz cornflour*

For topping:
3 *pineapple slices*
whipped cream
juice of half a large orange
glace cherries

For filling:
1 *medium tin pineapple*
   slices

Mix oil, water and egg yolks together in a bowl. Add flour, cornflour, baking powder, salt and 4 oz sugar, previously sifted. Beat well to form a smooth batter. Beat whites of eggs to a foam then beat in 2 oz sugar until mixture is stiff. Fold into batter and pour into two greased 8″ sandwich tins and bake in a fairly hot oven (400-425 F, Gas mark 6½-7) for 25 minutes. Turn out and allow to cool before filling and topping. For the filling, drain the pineapple slices and heat their juice with the orange juice. Mix the cornflour, sugar and egg yolk and stir into the fruit juices, allowing to boil for about three minutes and stirring constantly to avoid burning. Keep three good sized pineapple slices for the topping. Chop the rest and stir into the cooked juice mixture. Cool thoroughly before spreading on sandwich. Cover cake with the following topping. Whip cream stiffly, add orange juice to taste and a crushed pineapple slice. Whip once more before icing cake and decorating with remaining halved pineapple slices and glace cherries.

Mr Rowley's Salad
Spanish Cod
French Open Tart

MR ROWLEY'S SALAD

This is a very unusual starter; and Mr McFee, who first introduced it to Crossroads, insists that it was invented by a certain 'Anthony Rowley', because the ingredients include gammon and spinach. . . . But McFee has a very odd sense of humour. However it got its name, it's delicious – and surprisingly filling.

a dozen or more leaves of fresh, raw spinach	*1 ripe avocado pear*
2 oz button mushrooms	*2 gammon rashers*

Grill the rashers lightly, then chop them into thin matchsticks.

Use small, young leaves of spinach, tearing them off the stalks, and throw the stalks away.

Wash the spinach in several changes of water to remove the grit. Peel the avocado, remove the stone and dice the flesh. Wash and slice the raw mushrooms finely. Now combine all the ingredients (preferably while the chopped rashers are still warm) and toss well in the vinaigrette dressing which was described earlier under the recipe for 'Salade Niçoise'.

SPANISH COD

Is there anyone whose heart doesn't sink slightly at the sound of the word 'cod'? Poor fish – it seems to be nobody's best friend; but it will certainly win new admirers in this unusual Spanish fancy dress – again, of course, a legacy from the much-missed Carlos.

1½ lb cod fillet	*the juice and grated rind of*
3 slices brown bread	*one orange*
2 oz butter	*salt and pepper*
1 crushed clove of garlic	

Crumb the brown bread; melt the butter in a frying-pan, and add the crumbs, crushed garlic and grated orange rind. Stir well, until the breadcrumbs have soaked up all the butter. Now place the cod fillet in a buttered oven-dish, add salt and pepper, and give it a generous overcoat of breadcrumbs; then pour on the orange juice, last of all. Bake without a lid in a moderate oven (375 F, Gas mark 5) for 20 to 30 minutes. It's delicious with a really crisp salad and a few new potatoes.

FRENCH OPEN TART

Mr Booth learned the culinary arts after a long and hard apprenticeship as the lowest form of life in many large hotel kitchens, both here and on the continent. One of his great teachers was an elderly Swiss who was a 'maitre patissier' or master-pastry cook in Paris, and this recipe is one which Bernard Booth learned by watching him prepare it, many, many times.

For the pastry:
4 *oz flour*
a pinch of salt
2 *oz butter*
2 *oz castor sugar*
2 *egg yolks*

For the filling:
4 *oz butter*

4 *oz castor sugar*
2 *eggs*
4 *oz ground almonds*
1 *oz flour*

For the fruit:
3 *ripe pears, peaches, or*
    dessert apples
apricot jam

Make the pastry first; sieve the flour and salt on to the pastry board (Mr Booth's old master used a marble slab) and make a hole in the centre. Put the butter, sugar and egg yolks into this. Work these ingredients together in your fingertips, then gradually include the flour and continue to knead together until you have a smooth, light dough. Leave this in the fridge for at least an hour before you use it.

Fill in the time by peeling, coring or stoning, and thinly

slicing the fruit. Poach the slices for a few minutes in a light sugar syrup, then drain and allow to cool. Keep a little syrup aside for use later. Carry on and prepare the filling; soften the butter and cream with the sugar, using a wooden spoon, until it is fluffy. Beat in the eggs, one at a time, then add the ground almonds and flour, mixing well.

Now line a flan tin with the thinly-rolled pastry. Prick the bottom, and pour in the filling. Bake in a moderate oven (380 F, Gas mark 5) for about half an hour, then leave aside to cool. Now brush the surface with some apricot jam, thinned with a little sugar-syrup; then arrange the sliced fruit in a decorative pattern, overlapping in circles, and brush the slices with the remaining apricot glaze; then serve.

Chakchouka
Honey Glazed Gammon
Orange Charlotte

CHAKCHOUKA

When Meg Richardson went out to Tunisia to organise the opening of a hotel, she was fascinated not only by the beautiful beaches and the mysterious markets but also by Tunisia's national cuisine. Here is a dish she particularly enjoyed.

4 *or* 5 *onions*	1 *clove of garlic*
4 *green peppers and* 1 *red*	4 *or* 5 *tomatoes*
pepper	4 *eggs*
oil	

First slice and brown the onions in oil. When well browned, add the same number of sliced and de-seeded tomatoes, together with three or four sliced green peppers, one small sweet red pepper and a finely chopped clove of garlic. Simmer this until the vegetables are reduced to a pulp. Put this mixture into individual pottery casseroles, break an egg on to each, put into a moderate (350 F, Gas mark 4) oven and serve when the egg has set; about ten minutes.

HONEY-GLAZED GAMMON
This recipe deserves full marks; it has so many good points. For one thing, it looks glamorous and exciting and makes an excellent centrepiece for a celebration dinner. For another, after you've tried it hot from the oven, you can put the joint away to keep, because it's every bit as good sliced cold with salad. And last but not least – we've never yet come across anyone who didn't ask for a second helping!

1 *corner piece of gammon* (*about 3½ lb*)	1 *teaspoon French mustard*
2 *tablespoons clear honey*	1 *tin pineapple cubes*
2 *oz brown sugar*	

When you get the gammon from your grocer (and let's hope, as it's the awkward corner he can't slice into rashers, he won't charge you bacon prices!) you'll find that you need to soak it overnight to get out some of the salt, in a pan of cold water. Next day, drain off the water and fill up again with fresh. Put it on the stove and bring to the boil, then lower the heat, cover with a lid, and let it simmer. The cooking time will be 25 minutes per lb or part of a lb, and 25 minutes over. (So if it does weigh 3½ lb, it will simmer for 2 hours 5 minutes altogether.) If the water starts to boil away, keep the level topped up.

When it is cooked, take the gammon out of the saucepan to drain, then with a sharp knife cut off the coarse outside rind. On the fat that is left, make a chessboard pattern by drawing parallel knife cuts, first vertically and then horizontally. Now put the joint in an oven tin. Meanwhile, you will have made the honey glaze, blending together the honey, sugar and mustard in a small bowl. Now spread this all over the surface of the gammon – most particularly on the fat. Bake in a hot oven (400 F, Gas mark 6) for 20 minutes, basting as the melting glaze runs down into the pan.

To serve – place the joint on a carving-dish, and on the side you have marked out as the chessboard, stick a cube of pineapple with a wooden cocktail stick into every alternate square – the 'black' squares on the board, so to speak. Bring to the table, and carve in generous slices; ignoring those guests who say (and someone certainly will) 'Oh, it seems a shame to cut it up. . . .'

ORANGE CHARLOTTE

Another of Glenda's favourites – and because of the sugar and cream involved, it can't really be recommended when she's on one of her dieting jags. But Glenda (who has an answer for everything) defends her weakness by saying that it's got so much fruit and vitamin C in it, it simply *must* be fantastically good for you. . . . Just what the doctor ordered, in fact.

2 *oranges*	2 *tablespoons water*
1 *lemon*	½ *pint double cream*
1 *tin mandarins*	1 *portion fresh fruit salad –*
3 *egg whites*	*sliced apple, pear,*
½ *lb castor sugar*	*banana, cherries, etc*
½ *oz powdered gelatine*	

First, squeeze the juice from the oranges and lemon, adding the pulp of one of the oranges. Put the juice and pulp into a saucepan with the sugar, gelatine and water. Heat, stirring occasionally, until the gelatine dissolves, and put in the fridge to cool.

Wash out a ring mould – or if you haven't got one, use an ordinary pudding basin – and line it with the mandarin segments, not on their sides but with their inside edges pointing upward. When the gelatine mixture is just beginning to set, whisk it until it is frothy, then fold in the stiffly-whisked egg whites. Whip the cream thickly, and fold threequarters of this into the mixture as well. Now pour into the mould and return to the fridge to set.

To serve, turn the charlotte out of the mould and fill the centre with the fresh fruit mixture. (Or, if you're using a pudding-basin, make a ring of fresh fruit around the base.) Finish off with the remainder of the whipped cream in a decorative swirl on the top.

Herrings in Sour Cream
Romany Rabbit
Bakewell Tart

HERRINGS IN SOUR CREAM

Gus Harmon first came across this dish when his ship was in Copenhagen. He asked the proprietor of the restaurant for the recipe and here it is.

1 *lb salted herrings*	1 *cupful sour cream*
1 *medium onion finely*	*the juice of one lemon*
chopped	1 *dessert spoon sugar*
1 *cupful chopped apple*	*chopped parsley or chives*

Soak herrings for two days, changing water frequently. Fillet the herrings, remove skin and cut into one inch squares. Mix apple and onion into sour cream and add the lemon juice and sugar to taste.

Pour this mixture over the herrings and allow two or three hours for the flavours to intermingle before serving, garnishing with parsley or chives.

ROMANY RABBIT

'Romany' – meaning gypsy – might imply that the rabbit used in this recipe had disappeared one dark night into a poacher's pocket, but since the recipe came to Crossroads by way of old Sam Carne, the ex-lock-keeper nightwatchman, and as honest as the day is long, we would hesitate to cast any slur on Carney's reputation!

1 *rabbit, quartered into*
  joints
2 *oz butter*
2 *tablespoons cooking oil*
2 *tablespoons gin*
¼ *pint cider*

4 *tomatoes*
1 *large cooking apple*
½ *teaspoon curry powder*
¼ *lb mushrooms*
salt, pepper, mixed herbs

Put the oil and butter into a stewpan and brown the rabbit joints on all sides. Now warm the gin in a ladle and set it alight; pour this, still flaming, over the meat, and when the flames are out, add the cider; then the tomatoes (skinned and chopped) and the apple (peeled, cored and sliced). Sprinkle with salt, pepper, mixed herbs and curry powder; cover the pan and cook very slowly, letting the liquid simmer over a low flame for about an hour. Meanwhile, saute the sliced and washed mushrooms in a little butter, and add these at the last moment before dishing up.

BAKEWELL TART

Some people say that the *real* Bakewell tarts contain a rich butter and egg custard and no almonds. However, Jane Smith has an aunt who lives in Bakewell in Derbyshire and she insists that this is the proper way to make it.

6 *oz short crust pastry*
raspberry jam
3 *oz butter*
3 *oz sugar*
3 *oz fine bread or cake*
  crumbs

2 *eggs*
3 *oz ground almonds*
1 *or 2 drops almond essence*
icing sugar

Roll out pastry and line a pie plate, flan case or sandwich tin with it. Spread with a layer of raspberry jam. Cream butter and sugar together then add beaten eggs by degrees, beating very thoroughly. Still beating, add the almond essence, flour, cake or breadcrumbs and ground almonds in that order. When well mixed, spread over jam and bake tart in

centre of moderately hot oven (400 F, Gas mark 6) for 30
to 40 minutes until well risen and brown with the filling set.
Dredge with icing sugar.

Prawns with Aioli
Boeuf en Croute
Chiffon Pie

PRAWNS WITH AIOLI

And what, you may ask, is 'Aioli'? The answer is a kind of
garlic mayonnaise – and you've really got to love garlic to
get the best out of this one! If you're not too sure about it,
take our advice and steer well clear . . . but if you're an
addict, this one is just for you.

4 *oz peeled prawns, or scampi*	2 *egg yolks*
2 *cloves garlic*	½ *pint olive oil*
½ *teaspoonful salt*	*juice of half a lemon*

Wash the prawns and put them in the fridge to chill. Next
make the 'aioli'; crush the garlic with salt and pound
together into a paste, beating in the egg yolks. Now carry on
as if you were making a mayonnaise – adding the oil a drop
at a time, then a little more as it is absorbed. When half the
oil is used up, add the lemon juice – again, going carefully
and by degrees – then continue with the remaining oil. Now
serve the aioli in a small dish with the chilled prawns
arranged round the edge, and let your guests eat them in
their fingers, dipping into the garlicky sauce each time.

BOEUF EN CROUTE

Let's face it – any recipe that demands fillet steak is going to
be expensive, and nobody is going to claim that this is an
economical dish. But every now and again you might have a
special occasion when you feel like breaking out and saying

'Hang the expense. . . .' And you can guarantee that this will provide a meal that your guests are going to remember for a long, long time.

> ½ lb frozen puff pastry (or make your own, if you're feeling energetic!)
> 1½-2 lb fillet of beef – all in one piece
> a small tin of liver pate
> ½ lb button mushrooms
> 2 oz butter
> salt and pepper

Trim the steak, then roll out your pastry until it's thin enough and wide enough to wrap completely round the meat as if you were packing up a parcel. Spread the fillet with the butter, and then spread a layer of liver pate down the centre of the pastry, adding a line of mushrooms on top, plus salt and pepper. Put the steak on to the mushrooms, topping it with the rest of the pate and any remaining mushrooms, plus a little more seasoning. Now gift-wrap the whole thing by bringing up the edges of the pastry and sealing them tightly together (moisten with a little milk if it's being difficult) and decorate the resulting ridge on top with a pattern of knife-slashes. Put it in a baking-tin, in a pre-heated oven (425 F, Gas mark 7) and cook for twenty minutes. Cover it with foil if it starts to brown too quickly. After the twenty minutes are up, take out the baking-tin and reduce the heat to 350 F, Gas mark 4. Brush the pastry with milk to glaze it, replace the foil, and return to the cooling oven for another twenty five minutes. The total cooking-time is therefore 45 minutes – and this will give you a rare steak inside the crust; if you like your steak well done, leave it ten minutes longer still. Then dish up, cutting generous slices crosswise through the pastry – and wait for your guests' compliments!

CHIFFON PIE

Following Shughie McFee's abrupt departure from the Motel (after an alcoholic Hogmanay in Glasgow, when he awoke to find that he'd signed on as a ship's cook for a six-month voyage) his place was taken by Mrs Rawlings. This good lady had a special flair for sweets – some of her best specialities are still referred to as 'Mrs R's puds'. And here's one of them. It uses a mixture of blackberry and apple, but of course you could experiment with other fruit.

½ lb digestive biscuits	4 oz sugar
2 oz butter	½ pint cream
½ lb peeled, sliced cooking apples	½ oz gelatine
	1 tablespoon water
1 lb blackberries	

Make the crust first of all, by crushing the biscuits finely (using a rolling-pin and a clean tea-cloth) and mixing the melted butter in to bind them. Then press the mixture out to line a plate-pie dish.

To make the filling, cook the apples and most of the blackberries (keeping back about a dozen for decoration) with half the sugar, until they are soft. Sieve or whisk in a blender, to make a smooth puree. Now whisk the cream until it is stiff; using half of it (and keeping the rest aside for decoration) to fold into the fruit puree. Stir the gelatine into the hot water, allow it to dissolve completely, and let it cool; then stir into the mixture, adding the rest of the sugar at this stage. Pour the whole lot into the biscuit crust and allow to set.

Decorate by piping rosettes of the remaining whipped cream all round the edge, dotting here and there with blackberries.

English Taramasalata
Creamed Scampi
Profiterolles

ENGLISH TARAMASALATA

Have you tried the original Greek taramasalata – that piquant and fluffy pate made from smoked cods' roe? Whether you have or not, you'll enjoy making – and tasting! – this Crossroads equivalent; try serving it as an original first course, with plenty of hot toast to spread it on. You may have to search for smoked mackerel in some of your local delicatessens, but it's well worth the effort.

6 oz smoked mackerel (one or two, depending on their size)
2 slices of white bread, without the crusts
1 gill olive oil
juice of half a lemon, salt and black pepper
1 teaspoon of grated raw onion (or reconstituted onion flakes)
1 crushed clove of garlic
1 tablespoon of sour cream

Soften the bread by dipping it in warm water, then squeeze it out until it's just moist. Take the skin and all the bones from the mackerel, and pound it into a smooth paste, adding the bread. (A liquidiser saves a lot of trouble at this stage.) Now drip in the olive oil very slowly, as you carry on beating, as if you were making mayonnaise. When half the oil is used up, pour in the rest with the lemon juice and continue beating until the mixture thickens. Now add the onion, garlic and sour cream, with the salt and pepper to taste; then put it in the fridge to chill before you serve it.

CREAMED SCAMPI

Most people think of scampi served in the usual way, fried in breadcrumbs; but here is an alternative recipe which is really mouth-watering. Even Mrs Witton, who said she 'wasn't that struck on fishy things as a rule' made an exception in favour of this, the first time she tried it.

½ lb scampi – the 'jumbo'-
    sized kind, if possible
2 oz butter
1 oz flour
½ pint single cream

1 lemon, plus an extra dash
    of lemon juice
salt, pepper, and paprika
chopped chives and hot
    toast as a garnish

Melt the butter in a heavy frying-pan, toss the scampi in seasoned flour, and fry for about five minutes. Make sure they don't stick; add a little more butter if necessary. Now pour in the cream, stirring all the time, to make a smooth sauce. Add salt, pepper, paprika, and a dash of lemon juice. Put on to a serving-dish, surrounded by alternate triangles of hot toast and the lemon cut longways into thin wedges. Sprinkle chopped chives on top, and serve.

PROFITEROLLES

An unlikely and rather off-putting name for one of the most popular sweets in the entire Crossroads repertoire. Never mind what it's called – it's really a dish piled with tiny cream buns covered in chocolate sauce. Meg says she never eats sweets or chocolate nowadays – but it's very odd that she often happens to be in the kitchen just as the profiterolles are being dished up . . . and then of course she has to sample one – or even two – just to make sure they're up to standard, doesn't she?

For the pastry:
2 oz plain flour
1½ oz butter
2 eggs
¼ pint water

For the sauce:
¼ lb plain chocolate

4 oz castor sugar
1 dessertspoon instant
    coffee
¼ pint water

For the filling:
¼ pint double cream

First make the pastry: the kind you use for cream buns, known in the trade as 'choux pastry'. Sift the flour on to a piece of paper. Heat the butter and water together in a saucepan, bring to the boil, then take from the heat and tip in all the flour at once, as fast as possible. Beat with a wooden spoon until the mixture leaves the sides of the pan clean. Set aside to cool.

Beat the eggs, and when the paste has cooled, add these gradually, still using the wooden spoon. It's hard work to mix the whole thing in smoothly, but persevere!

Grease a baking-sheet lightly, and drop teaspoonfuls of the mixture on to it – about an inch apart, to give them room to rise and spread. Cook in a hot oven (450 F, Gas mark 8) for about half an hour, until they are quite firm. Then slice them in half, scraping out any uncooked paste left inside, and leave them on a wire rack to cool.

Now whip the cream until it is stiff. When the pastry shells are quite cold, fill each one with cream, sticking the halves back together. Make the sauce by melting all the ingredients over a low heat; when the chocolate has melted, bring it to the boil and cook briskly for five minutes. Let it cool, then pour over the profiterolles, built up in a pyramid.

Moules Marinieres
Pork Chops Normandes
French Pancakes (*Crepes*)

MOULES MARINIERES
A classic French dish, very much favoured by Mr Lovejoy when he was in charge of the kitchen – and it's won so many admirers over the years that Mr Booth has had to learn to make it in the selfsame way. . . . But, as he admits, the mark of a really great mind is one's readiness to learn!

1 *small onion, 1 clove of garlic, both chopped finely*
2 *oz butter, chopped into small pieces and rolled in flour*
4 *pints of mussels*

1 *glass of dry white wine; and double this quantity of water*
black pepper
a sprig of thyme and some chopped parsley – fresh from the garden, if possible!

Put the wine, water, onion, garlic and seasoning into a large saucepan and let it simmer until it has reduced to about two-thirds, then add the scrubbed mussels. Raise the flame under the pan until it is bubbling briskly, and put the lid on. As soon as the shells are open, remove the mussels and keep them hot in a deep serving dish. Now add the floured butter to the liquor and heat until the butter has melted. Then pour it over the mussels, sprinkle with chopped parsley, and serve.

The French method (so Isabelle Zola taught us when she came to stay at the Motel) of tackling mussels is this: after you've eaten the first one, use the empty open shell like a pair of pincers to extract all the remaining mussels from their shells. . . . But however you do it, you'll need a finger-bowl afterwards!

PORK CHOPS NORMANDES

Mr McFee's theory is that the Scots and the French have many qualities in common. (They even have some similar words – the Scots 'ashet' for a saucer is not unlike the French 'assiette'.) And much to Mr Booth's annoyance, McFee insists that this proves that the Scots, like the French, provide the master-chefs for the other races of the world.

Whether that's true or not (and in the case of most of McFee's statements, you need to take them with a whole Siberian mineful of salt!) here is a French recipe that anyone can make – a dish from Normandy, the home of apples and dairy-farms, cider and cream.

4 *pork chops*	2 *cooking apples*
1 *oz butter*	4 *dessertspoons of brown*
1 *wineglass of cider*	*sugar*
1 *small carton of sour*	1 *pinch of sage*
cream	*salt and pepper*

Trim the rinds and some of the fat from the chops, and brown them on both sides in the melted butter. Put the chops into a casserole, then add the cider to the hot fat, turn off the heat, and stir in the sour cream. Add the salt, pepper and sage. Now peel and core the apples and cut them across into halves. Put a half apple on each chop, pour the cream sauce over them, and finish by covering each apple-half with brown sugar. Put on the casserole lid and bake at 350 F, Gas mark 4 for about threequarters of an hour.

FRENCH PANCAKES (CREPES)

These pancakes are richer and thinner than the English pancake. They can be served in many ways and it is worth remembering that they can be frozen but Bernard Booth says that you must remember to separate each pancake with a sheet of greaseproof paper.

$\frac{1}{2}$ *lb flour*	$\frac{3}{4}$ *pint of milk*
1 *oz sugar*	2 *tablespoons corn oil*
a pinch of salt	2 *tablespoons brandy*
3 *eggs*	

Sift together flour, sugar and salt. Beat the eggs and add them to the dry ingredients. Still beating, add milk, oil and brandy. Leave to stand (after pouring through fine sieve) for two hours or more. The batter should have a cream-like consistency and may be thinned with a little water if necessary.

To cook, heat a heavy frying pan 5-6″ in diameter, brushed with very little oil or butter. Pour in about two tablespoons of batter and swirl pan so that the whole of the bottom is covered thinly. Cook until golden then toss or turn; about one minute each side. Stack on plate until all are cooked. Suggested fillings: apple puree, jam, marmalade, soft cream cheese.

Huevos a la Flamenco
Sweet and Sour Pork
Brown Betty

HUEVOS A LA FLAMENCO
This was another of the dishes that Carlos introduced at Crossroads. You really could call it the Spanish version of eggs and bacon, because if you do not have a handy delicatessen it is possible to substitute gammon rashers for the Spanish ham. It is fairly filling, so it is wise to follow it with a light main course. In fact Avis Warren told us she often made it as a late night supper dish when she and Bill came back from work.

6 *eggs*
3 *tomatoes, sliced*
2 *large red peppers*
3 *slices of dried Spanish ham, chopped*
6 *slices of pork sausage*
½ *cup of cooked peas*
½ *cup of cooked French beans*
1 *large onion, sliced*
2 *cloves garlic, chopped*
salt and pepper
1 *teaspoon chopped parsley*
oil

Soften the garlic and onion in the oil and then add the ham and tomatoes. When these are cooked add the peas, beans and sausage. Cook until sausage is done. Add salt and pepper to taste.
Divide into three parts and place in three small oven plates. Break two eggs over each oven plate, surround with peppers and heat in oven until eggs are set. Sprinkle chopped parsley over the top to serve.
Serves 3

SWEET AND SOUR PORK

Wonder of wonders, here's a really cheap recipe – and yet one that is unusual and even a little exotic. Whether it really hails from the mystic orient, we wouldn't like to say; but the one thing certain is that it has a delicious flavour all of its own – and it's amazingly easy to cook.

1 lb lean pork (pork belly is economical, as long as it isn't too fatty)	2 tablespoons vinegar
	1 wineglass dry sherry
	2 tablespoons soy sauce
2 tablespoons clear honey	1 tablespoon cornflour

Mix all the liquid ingredients in a casserole, stirring well until the honey has dissolved, and then cut the pork into strips and put the meat into the liquid, leaving overnight to marinate.

Next day put the casserole into the oven and cook at 375 F, Gas mark 5 for 1¼ hours. Then, in a small saucepan, mix together the cornflour and one tablespoon of the hot sauce from the casserole, stirring until it has blended smoothly. Gradually add all the rest of the sauce until it thickens at boiling-point, then pour it back over the meat in the casserole and dish up. It's particularly good served with rice and a green salad.

BROWN BETTY

This is another of Mrs Rawlings's old-fashioned English recipes. Goodness only knows how it got its name – who was Betty, and was she really a brunette? Well, frankly, it couldn't matter less; it's a delicious and filling pudding – and if you want a change, you can serve it cold instead of hot, cut into slices and smothered in whipped cream.

4 oz butter	grated rind and juice of 1 lemon
8 oz white breadcrumbs	
4 oz soft brown sugar	1½ lb cooking apples
½ level teaspoon ground cinnamon	1 teacup of hot water

Melt the butter gently in a saucepan. Take it from the heat and stir in the breadcrumbs. Then mix separately in a small basin the brown sugar, cinnamon and the grated lemon rind and juice. Peel, core and slice the apples.

Butter a baking-dish generously, then make a layer of one-third of the buttered crumbs; cover this with a layer of apple slices, and then sprinkle with the sugar mixture. Repeat these three layers, and finish off with the last third of the breadcrumbs.

Cover with foil or greaseproof paper and bake in the centre of the oven (350 F, Gas mark 4) for 25 minutes. Remove the foil or paper and continue to bake for another half-hour, until the top is crisp and brown.

Trout with Almonds
Gammon Steaks in Cider
Pears Belle Helene

TROUT WITH ALMONDS

Local poacher and ne'er-do-well Archie Gibbs learned how to tickle trout when he was a boy – he was a proper little joker even in those days! Nowadays the Crossroads Motel gets its supplies from a trout farm not too far away. You can use frozen trout for this dish and, incidentally, trout is one of the few fish that does not suffer from freezing.

4 *trout* (1 *per person*)   1½ *oz flaked almonds*
flour, pepper and salt   *lemon wedges*
3 *oz butter*

Ask your fishmonger to gut the fish through the gills. Roll them in seasoned flour and fry in half the butter until they are cooked, golden and crisp – about five minutes each side – taking special care that they don't stick to the pan. Remove, put on a hot plate, sprinkle with lemon juice and keep warm. Add the rest of the butter to the pan and fry the blanched flaked almonds golden brown. Then pour them, with the butter, over the trout and serve immediately.

GAMMON STEAKS IN CIDER
How about something simple for a change? Faye Mansfield started out as such an inexperienced cook that (in Avis's phrase) she couldn't boil water without burning it. . . . But she was determined to learn, and buckled down to the task, going to cookery classes and picking up tips from the Motel chefs. Mr Booth kindly passed on this very straightforward recipe, and she tried it the same night at the girls' basement flat – with instant success.

2 *cooking apples*	4 *gammon steaks*
2 *oz butter*	$\frac{1}{4}$ *pint dry cider*

Peel, core and skin the apples; then fry the gammon steaks in the butter until they are golden brown on both sides. Put the steaks into a casserole, and fry the sliced apple lightly, adding these to the casserole in turn. Pour over the cider, put the lid on, and let it cook for about threequarters of an hour at 350 F, Gas mark 4.

PEARS BELLE HELENE
Until recently, Jill and Stan didn't often give dinner parties; they couldn't afford lavish entertaining, and Jill found that looking after Sarah-Jane, plus her part-time job of home-dressmaking, took up a lot of time. But nowadays, when they invite friends round for a meal, this is a simple but simply perfect dessert which Jill loves to make. (And if there's a portion left over – young Sarah-Jane is very helpful about polishing it off.)

4 *ripe pears (or 8 tinned halves of pear)*	*dash of lemon juice*
	vanilla ice-cream
$\frac{1}{2}$ *pint water*	*hot chocolate sauce (either*
8 *oz sugar*	*bought ready-made or*
vanilla essence	*made at home)*

If you're using fresh pears, peel, core and halve them. Then make a syrup with the water, sugar, vanilla essence and lemon juice – and when the sugar has melted, poach the pears in this syrup for three or four minutes. Dish up, allowing two half-pears to each guest, and one scoop of ice-cream. Pour over the hot chocolate sauce and serve.

Real Mushroom Soup
Shepherds Pie
Cabinet Pudding

REAL MUSHROOM SOUP

You've already seen Sandy's comments about tinned tomato soup, as opposed to the real home-made variety; goodness knows that this applies even more to the Crossroads mushroom soup. There really is no comparison! Just try it and see.

½ lb mushrooms	½ pint milk
1 medium-sized onion	3 tablespoons cream
2 oz butter	1 oz flour
¾ pint chicken stock	salt and pepper to taste

Wash and slice the mushrooms; peel and chop the onion. Melt 1 oz of butter in a heavy saucepan and add the vegetables. Cover and simmer for about ten minutes, until the juices run. Add the stock, bring to the boil, then simmer for ten more minutes. Now pass it through a sieve, or blend in the liquidiser.

Then melt the other ounce of butter in the bottom of the saucepan, and stir in the flour, until it has cooked gently (about one minute). Pour in the milk, a little at a time, stirring all the while, and make a thin, smooth sauce. Bring to the boil and simmer for a few minutes, adding salt and pepper. Now stir in the mushroom mixture, and heat to just below boiling point. Remove from the stove, and stir in the cream before serving.

SHEPHERDS PIE

Strictly speaking Shepherds Pie should be made from mutton or lamb and, if other meats are used, it should be called Cottage Pie. Whatever is used, it is best made with raw meat and is an economical way of presenting a tasty meal from the cheaper cuts. This is the way Mrs Ash used to make it for Sandy on the farm, a long time ago.

1 *large onion, chopped*
3 *cloves garlic, chopped*
3 *tablespoons oil*
1 *lb beef, chuck or shin, minced*
1 *tablespoon tomato puree*
¼ *pint dry cider*
½ *pint beef stock*
3 *heaped teaspoons cornflour*
salt and freshly ground pepper
2-3 *lbs potatoes*
2½ *oz butter*
½ *pint milk*
1 *oz grated cheese*
1 *tablespoon parmesan*

Melt onion and garlic in oil until soft; raise heat and add meat, stirring until browned. Add tomato puree, cider and half the stock. Mix cornflour with remaining stock, pour into pan, stir well, season and simmer for ten minutes covered. Meanwhile boil potatoes in their skins, peel and mash them with the butter and milk. Put the mince into a large dish and cover with mashed potato. Fork it up into an attractive pattern and sprinkle with cheese. Bake for 15 minutes at 400 F, Gas mark 6 then reduce heat to 350 F, Gas mark 4 and bake for a further ¾ hour.

CABINET PUDDING

In these days of instant food, puddings and sweets are often hacked off a block, thawed out or, after just adding milk, whipped to a froth and a frenzy before being topped with 'wonderfoam' or some other product of a laboratory trying to be a dairy. Many Victorian puddings were produced from 'left overs' from a previous tea party. 'If you haven't given your teatime guests sponge cake and ratafias it is worth

going out to buy them,' said Vi Blundell whose recipe for
such a pudding is given below.

2 *sponge cakes*	**For decoration:**
3 *ratafia biscuits*	*glace cherries and angelica,*
2 *eggs*	*raspberry jam*
½ *pint milk*	
1 *oz sugar*	
vanilla essence	

Cut the sponge cake into dice and crumble the ratafias. Beat
the eggs with the sugar, add the milk, heated but not boiling,
and the vanilla flavouring. Pour this over the cake and soak
till quite cold.

Grease a plain mould. Put a round of greaseproof paper in
the bottom of the mould and decorate with pieces of cherry
and angelica. Pour the mixture into this and steam gently
until firm – from threequarters to one hour. Turn out of the
mould and pour hot raspberry jam round.

Cream Cheese & Cucumber Mousse
Kidneys in Wine Sauce
Baba au Rhum

CREAM CHEESE AND CUCUMBER MOUSSE
Kate Evans – Jane Smith's Salvation Army friend – went on
a health-food kick when she was going out with Buzz
Dawkins; but although all the ingredients of this recipe are
very healthy indeed, she never tasted anything quite so
delicious as this light, creamy mousse. . .

1 *cucumber*	½ *oz gelatine (or the*
1 *large carton cottage*	*contents of 1 envelope of*
cheese	*powdered gelatine)*
¼ *pint chicken stock*	¼ *pint whipped double cream*
	chopped chives for
	garnishing

Peel the cucumber and remove the seeds; then chop it up finely. Leave it sprinkled with salt for about an hour, to draw out any excess moisture. Now pass the cottage cheese through a sieve, and combine it with the chopped cucumber. Dissolve the gelatine in half the chicken stock, and then add the remaining stock and leave it until it starts to set. When it is beginning to 'gell', mix into the cheese and cucumber mixture. Put this in the fridge to chill, and just before serving, stir in the whipped cream; then as a final touch, garnish generously with the chopped chives.

KIDNEYS IN WINE SAUCE

When Carole Hewson moved into her new flat, one of the first meals she cooked there was supper for two – herself and Simon Whitaker. And this is the recipe she prepared for him.

1 lb lamb's kidneys	1 bay leaf
1½ oz butter	salt and pepper
1 tablespoon olive oil	small cup of beef stock
1 small onion, chopped finely	small cup of red wine
1 clove garlic, crushed	1 teaspoon concentrated tomato paste
2½ tablespoons flour	4 tomatoes peeled, seeded and chopped
¼ lb finely sliced small mushrooms	4 dashes Worcester sauce
a good pinch each of basil and thyme	finely chopped parsley
a small pinch oregano	cooked long-grain rice

Skin and core the kidneys before cutting into reasonably thick slices.

Heat oil and butter in large frying pan, then fry onion and garlic until light gold in colour, about five minutes. Add the kidneys, stirring constantly for a further five minutes. Take kidneys, drained, from the pan and keep warm. Sprinkle flour into pan, stirring, and add mushrooms, seasoning and herbs before gradually adding stock and wine. Bring to boil, lower heat and simmer, uncovered, for about ten minutes. Add remaining ingredients and the kidneys. Stir and heat for a further three minutes and serve on a bed of hot, long-grained rice.

BABA AU RHUM

Here is Bernard Booth's recipe for a great French classical pudding for that very special occasion – it is delicious!

¼ lb plain flour
1 teaspoon castor sugar
2 small eggs
3-4 tablespoons milk
¼ oz yeast
2½ oz butter
1 oz currants

For the syrup:
½ lb sugar
½ pint water
6 tablespoons rum

Sieve warmed flour with the sugar. Cream the yeast with a little of the warmed milk. Mix with the rest of the milk and the beaten egg. Beat this into the flour for five minutes to make a thick batter.

Cover bowl and allow to rise for about 40 minutes. Cut the butter into small pats and beat it, with the currants, into the batter.

Pour the batter into 6 or 8 large dariole moulds or one ring mould. They should be only half full. Allow batter to prove in a warm place until it has doubled in size. Bake at 425 F, Gas mark 6-7 until very light and crisp on top; for small tins 15-20 minutes – for a large one 30 minutes.

Turn out of tins and prick all over with a skewer before basting with hot syrup, made as follows:

Combine ½ lb sugar with ½ pint of water in a saucepan. Simmer gently until it thickens, then stir in 6 tablespoons of rum.

MENUS FOR WINTER

Spinach Soup
Hungarian Goulash
Apple Strudel

SPINACH SOUP

When Jill and Stan Harvey have friends round for dinner, Jill often starts with a chilled soup as it can be prepared well in advance and leaves her more time to prepare her main course. This is one of her favourites.

12 oz frozen chopped spinach, cooked	3 tablespoons dry vermouth
1½ pints single cream	1 teaspoon grated lemon rind
2 chicken bouillon cubes	1 hard-boiled egg

Puree the cooked spinach in a blender. Dissolve bouillon cubes in heated cream and stir. Remove from heat. Add spinach, vermouth and lemon. Chill and serve garnished with chopped egg.

HUNGARIAN GOULASH

When they have come into the Motel after a long drive on a wet and cold day, the Crossroads customers nearly all plump for Hungarian Goulash if it is on the menu. One of the beauties of this dish, if you are preparing it at home, is that it is better reheated, as are most dishes containing wine.

1 lb beef (rump)	butter
1 carrot	2 onions
2 teaspoons paprika	1 heaped tablespoon flour
salt and a pinch of pepper	1 gill red wine
1 pinch carraway seeds	bouquet garni
1 gill of tomato sauce	1 clove garlic, finely chopped
2 gills hot beef stock	
1 teaspoon chopped parsley	

Cut meat into two-inch cubes, brown them in butter then add sliced carrot, chopped onion and the paprika. Cook for a few minutes then dredge with flour and moisten with stock and wine, stirring constantly. Add the bouquet garni, carraway seeds, tomato sauce, salt and a little pepper. Cook slowly for an hour before adding the minced garlic and parsley. Simmer until meat is tender, and serve with boiled noodles.

APPLE STRUDEL

The most important part of this famous European delicacy is the dough. It requires patience and practice. Mr Lovejoy had both. He made a melt-in-the-mouth strudel in the following way.

2 *tablespoons corn oil*	**For the filling:**
10 *oz plain flour*	*about 1 lb cooking apples,*
1 *well-beaten egg*	*peeled, cored and thinly*
a good pinch of salt	*sliced.*
a little lukewarm water	2 *oz chopped nuts*
2½ *oz butter or margarine*	1 *teaspoon mixed spice*
2 *tablespoons breadcrumbs*	*sultanas*

Sieve flour and salt together, make a well in the centre. Work in oil from centre then add the egg and enough water to make a firm dough.

Knead well taking the dough in your hand and beat it against the board until it shows bubbles and comes cleanly off your hand and the board.

Form into one or two lumps, cover with a warm cloth and leave aside for thirty minutes. Spread a large cloth on a table, flour it lightly, then begin to roll and pull out the dough until it is as thin as paper and of uniform thickness. Leave a few minutes to dry on the table. Fry the bread-crumbs in the fat until brown then sprinkle over the strudel with a little of the fat brushed over it too. Arrange apples evenly on the surface leaving about an inch each side so that you can seal the ends. Then distribute other ingredients over the pastry. When covered with the filling, take the edge of the cloth and with a lifting movement roll up the strudel like a Swiss roll. Make into a horseshoe shape, if strudel is too long to fit on to a greased baking sheet. Brush top with a little butter. Bake in centre of hot oven (450 F, Gas mark 8) for twenty minutes then reduce to 375 F, Gas mark 5 for a further fifteen to twenty minutes. Serve hot or cold, liberally dredged with icing sugar.

Chicory and Ham
Pasta Perfection
Zabaglione

CHICORY AND HAM

When globe-trotting journalist Angela Kelly came to stay at the Motel, on one of her flying visits, she sometimes introduced the kitchen staff to unusual dishes from overseas. This one came after a trip to Brussels, and is a Belgian speciality which makes a warming starter to a cold day.

4 *heads of chicory*	1 *teacup grated cheese*
4 *thin slices of ham*	1 *tablespoonful of cream*
2 *oz butter*	*salt, pepper and*
1½ *oz flour*	*breadcrumbs*
½ *pint warm milk*	

First make a cheese sauce; melt the butter in a heavy saucepan and mix in the flour, stirring all the time. Gradually add the warm milk and keep stirring until it thickens. Now add the grated cheese and carry on stirring until it is blended in smoothly. Last of all, stir in the cream.

Meanwhile, simmer the chicory in salted water until it's just tender. Strain and dry, roll each chicory in a slice of ham, and place them side by side in an oven-dish. Pour the cheese sauce over them, and sprinkle with breadcrumbs. Then cook in a moderate oven (350 F, Gas mark 3-4) for twenty minutes. If they haven't browned enough, pop them under the grill for a few moments more.

PASTA PERFECTION

There may be one or two superficial resemblances between this recipe and the classic Spaghetti Bolognaise (on page 147) but when you've tasted them both, you'll see why this one deserves its nickname – 'perfection'.

Carlos Rafael was a Spaniard, but he knew a lot about all the cookery of the Mediterranean – and this rich Italian pasta was one of his specialities. How authentic it is, we wouldn't know; but some of the Motel's Italian guests have been very vocal in its praise. Admittedly, you'll need about an hour's cooking time to get it together – but who's going to quibble over sixty minutes, when the result is 'perfection'?

2 *tablespoons cooking oil*	*. . . and about ½ lb of*
1 *onion*	*boiled noodles, or*
1 *carrot*	*tagliatelle, or spaghetti –*
1 *stick of celery*	*whatever kind of pasta*
2 *oz streaky bacon*	*you prefer*
2 *oz chicken livers*	
½ *lb minced beef*	**For the sauce:**
¾ *pint beef stock*	1 *oz butter*
1 *tablespoon tomato puree*	1 *oz plain flour*
1 *tablespoon cornflour*	½ *pint milk*
salt and pepper	2 *oz grated cheese*

Boil the pasta as instructed on the packet, then drain and keep warm. While it is cooking, peel and slice the onion and carrot, chop the celery, and fry all these vegetables for a few minutes in the hot oil. Add the bacon and chicken livers, chopped up together, together with the mince, and fry until nicely browned. Add the tomato puree and then the stock, a little at a time; cover and leave to simmer for 30 minutes. Mix the cornflour with a little water to a smooth paste, and add to the mixture, stirring well; then bring to the boil and dash in salt and pepper to taste.

To make the sauce, melt the butter, add flour, and cook for one minute; take the pan from the stove and gradually add milk, stirring carefully until it has blended in. Return to the stove and bring to the boil, cooking for one minute until the sauce thickens.

Now, in an ovenproof dish, arrange a layer of pasta, then a layer of mince mixture, then one of white sauce; repeat the process layer by layer, and sprinkle the top with grated cheese. Bake in a hot oven (425 F, Gas mark 7) for twenty minutes, or until it is a golden brown.

ZABAGLIONE

A lot of nonsense is talked about this particular dessert; and it's true that if you let the mixture get too hot, the egg will curdle, and you might as well throw it away and give up! But if you take care, this really is a very straightforward and delicious sweet for a special occasion.

3 *egg yolks*
3 *tablespoons castor sugar*

1 *wineglass of marsala,*
   madeira or sweet sherry

Put the yolks and sugar into a basin and whisk. Add the wine slowly and continue to beat until it is blended in. Now put the basin over a small pan of boiling water and carry on beating as the mixture warms through – *not* letting it get too hot! When it rises into a creamy froth, pour into individual glasses and serve – ideally with ratafia biscuits or sponge fingers.

Napoleon Bean Salad
Beef & Prune Casserole
Danish Chocolate Cake

NAPOLEON BEAN SALAD

Diane Parker says she always used to feel sorry for poor old Napoleon, stuck away in exile on the Isle of Elba. . . . Until she tasted this recipe; and she decided that if this is what he had to eat, he couldn't have suffered *too* badly.

2 *large tins of kidney beans*   *French dressing*
1 *large tin of tuna fish*   *chopped parsley to garnish*
1 *large onion, sliced very*
  thinly into rings

Marinate the beans and onion rings in French dressing for about an hour. Add the flaked tuna fish to the beans and mix well. Garnish with parsley and serve on a bed of lettuce.

BEEF AND PRUNE CASSEROLE

Crossroads guests with really long memories might recall Mrs Violet Blundell (usually known as Vi) – the wife of farmhand Les, and a part-time char at the Motel. Her favourite lugubrious remark was 'It's all go, innit?' – and she generally looked on the gloomy side of life. But this was a recipe which she introduced to Meg, who tasted it, and commented that after all, dark clouds *do* have silver linings sometimes.

1½ *lb lean stewing-steak*   ¼ *pint beefstock*
flour, salt and pepper   1 *tablespoon tomato puree*
2 *tablespoons dripping*   ½ *lb prunes*
2 *onions*   *chopped parsley*
½ *lb young carrots*

Remove excess fat or gristle from the meat; cut into cubes and roll in seasoned flour. Fry in the dripping until well browned, and then place in a casserole. Fry the chopped onions until golden, and add these to the meat, together with finely-sliced carrots. Now stir a tablespoon of the seasoned flour into the hot fat and cook for a few moments, until it browns; then stir in the beefstock, a little at a time, and bring to the boil. Add more salt and pepper if necessary and stir in the tomato puree. Now pour this all into the casserole; put on a lid and cook in a slow oven (325 F, Gas mark 3) for 2½ hours.

Add the prunes to this dish either one hour before the end of the cooking time, if you're using ordinary prunes which you've soaked overnight (as Vi Blundell did) or half an hour if you're using 'them newfangled tenderised ones'. Sprinkle chopped parsley on top before you bring to the table.

DANISH CHOCOLATE CAKE

This is another of Kelly's trophies, brought back from an assignment overseas, when she had to go to Copenhagen to report on a Sex-Film Festival. She returned with the verdict that the Danish food was more exciting than any of the films – and this particular recipe has been in the Motel repertoire ever since. It's not over-sweet, with a crisp texture and an unexpectedly sophisticated flavour . . . which, come to think of it, is a pretty fair description of Angela Kelly herself.

½ lb plain chocolate	1 oz toasted flaked almonds
½ lb butter	1 oz shelled walnuts
2 egg yolks	2 oz glace cherries
½ lb digestive biscuits	double cream

To make this cake, you will need an 8″ or 9″ cake tin, with a removable base that pushes up and out; it's the only way to extricate the cake once it's made. (Incidentally, the recipe will make sufficient for eight good helpings; but you can serve some and keep the rest in the fridge till later.)

107

Line the cake-tin with kitchen foil. Break the chocolate up and melt over a gentle heat with the butter, then stir in the egg yolks. Now break the biscuits into small pieces and put in a mixing-bowl, together with the almonds and walnuts, crushed in a pestle and mortar (or with a rolling-pin, if you find it easier). Cut the cherries in half and add these, then pour in the chocolate mixture and stir well. Spoon it all into the lined cake tin, and refrigerate – preferably overnight – until the cake has hardened. Then slide up the base of the tin and peel off all the foil. To serve, cut up into fairly thin slices and pour a little cream over each portion.

Stuffed Mushrooms
Beef Stroganoff
Swiss Apple Tart

STUFFED MUSHROOMS
When the Crossroads kitchen is catering for a wedding reception or cocktail party, our older customers always ask for this savoury which was first created by Mr Lovejoy. It is very rich but quite delicious.

2 *doz medium to large mushrooms*	1 *onion, very finely chopped or minced*
4 *oz Danish Blue cheese*	*fine breadcrumbs*
4 *oz Philadelphia cheese*	*chopped parsley*

Wash and drain mushrooms and then parboil them for one minute.
Remove stems, mince these and make a paste with them by adding onion and the two kinds of cheese. Fill the mushroom caps with this paste and cover with breadcrumbs and parsley mixed. Place under a grill until hot and lightly browned.

BEEF STROGANOFF

If you use fillet steak – which you should do, in theory, for this recipe – you'll need to be a millionaire . . . and there aren't that many about nowadays. So as an alternative, ask your butcher for a cheaper cut of steak; when you explain how it's to be used (sliced up into tiny pieces) he may suggest, as the Kings Oak butcher suggested to Meg, using the tail end of the fillet, where it narrows down to a thin point, too small to sell for grilling. Meg also confesses to any sticklers for accuracy that this is a labour-saving and simplified version of 'Boeuf Stroganoff' – but she insists that it's hard to tell the difference.

1½ lbs beefsteak	½ lb butter (approximately)
3 onions	1 carton soured cream
¾ lb mushrooms	salt and pepper

Slice the steak thinly, each piece being about the size of a 50p piece. Peel and slice the onions, wash and slice the mushrooms. Fry the onion rings in a little butter until they are soft, then put them aside; add a little more butter and fry the mushrooms, then put these to keep warm with the onions. Fry the sliced steak, adding more butter as you need it, stirring and turning the meat until it is browned on both sides. Add salt and pepper; mix the onions and mushrooms back in, then pour on the sour cream. Stir up once more and bring to the boil – then serve at once.

SWISS APPLE TART

This was one of Granny Fraser's own recipes which Meg, Kitty and Andy adored as children. It became equally popular with the second generation and now Jill is already serving it up in her household. It is a very festive looking dish and it is usually put on the Crossroads menu around Christmas, New Year or for special functions. A note of warning – it is also very rich and second helpings for the smaller fry should be discouraged.

1¾ lb apples
½ lb mixed dried fruit
   (*sultanas, raisins,*
   currants)
4¼ oz butter or margarine
1½ teaspoons ground
   cinnamon
¼ lb brown sugar

½ lb flour
¼ teaspoon baking powder
2 oz castor sugar
1 egg yolk
½ cup milk
1 egg white
6 oz icing sugar

Peel and slice the apples. Turn the apples and dried fruit into a saucepan with ¼ oz of the fat and 1 teaspoon of the cinnamon. Add brown sugar, cover and stew until tender. Turn out on a plate to cool. Grease a tart tin or pie plate. Sift flour with baking powder, castor sugar and the rest of the cinnamon. Lightly run in the rest of the butter. Make into a dry, rather stiff dough with the beaten egg yolk diluted in the milk.

Divide the pastry into three portions. Roll out two rounds, one for the bottom and one for the cover, then roll a strip 1″ wide for the side. Line bottom of tin (or plate). Moisten edge with cold water, then fit strip round. Mould edges together. Add filling, brush edges of pastry with cold water and fit on cover. Bake in a fairly hot oven (425 F, Gas mark 7) for about ¾ hour. Stand till cool. Beat egg white till frothy, then add sifted icing sugar. When well blended and of a creamy consistency, spread icing over the top of tart.

Briks
Pork with Apples & Prunes
Chocolate Rum Cake

BRIKS

Briks – another Tunisian delicacy – are made from a very thin sheet of semolina dough which encases a savoury meat, egg or fish mixture and is then fried in hot oil. If you find your local grocer does not stock semolina flour, they are just as good made with puff pastry. Meg makes them like this:

Take a packet of frozen puff pastry and allow to thaw. Chop some meat, wash and chop some parsley: peel and mince a small onion. Mix together, adding salt and pepper to taste. Cook mixture in salted butter. Remove it from the stove and put the mixture through a fine mincer. Add some grated cheese and re-heat. Roll out some pastry thinly turning in the edge to make a 6″ square. In the centre put some of the meat mixture, break an egg over it and fold the square in half to form a triangle. Seal edges and slide into a pan of hot oil. Cook both sides until golden brown, drain and serve with slices of lemon.

There are many different fillings you can use for this dish. A favourite of Meg's is tuna fish, onion, parsley, and a dash of pepper and some capers.

Tinned sardines are an excellent filling also. They are cooked in exactly the same way as the meat is in the first recipe.

PORK WITH APPLES AND PRUNES

This is a good old farmhouse recipe which Diane first learned when she went to stay with her Auntie Peggy and Uncle Ed in Shropshire. On winter days, the wind blows meanly across those border hills, and Benny told Diane that this was one of his favourite dinners – 'cos it do keep the cold out.'

4 lean pork chops	8 prunes
1 oz dripping	¼ pint cider
2 cooking apples	¼ pint water
2 onions	rosemary, salt and pepper

Rub salt and pepper into the chops on both sides, and brown them in the hot dripping. Now peel and slice the apples and onions, and make a layer of each in a heavy oven casserole. Cook the prunes for a few minutes in boiling water; cut them in half, taking out the stones. Put half the prunes into the casserole, and then add the chops and sprinkle with rosemary. Cover with another layer of apple and onion, and then the rest of the prunes. Pour in the cider and water; put on a tight-fitting lid and cook at 350 F, Gas mark 4 for about two hours, adding a little more water later if it seems to be drying up.

CHOCOLATE RUM CAKE
Another dessert that has to be made in advance – which must be an advantage for a busy hostess. (Incidentally, although most of the recipes in this book are meant for four, this one will make enough cake for 6 or even 8 portions.)

David Hunter doesn't very often eat sweet things, but he makes an exception in the case of Chocolate Rum Cake; there is a wicked rumour that, one morning when he visited the kitchen very early for some reason, he discovered that one portion had been left over in the fridge – and had it, with a cup of black coffee, for his breakfast. If this is true, he must have been feeling particularly strong that day.

5 oz plain flour	½ teaspoon vanilla essence
1 oz cocoa	2 eggs
½ level teaspoon salt	6 tablespoons corn oil
2 level teaspoons baking powder	6 tablespoons milk
4 oz granulated sugar	2 tablespoons rum
¼ pint water	½ pint double cream
5 oz soft brown sugar	¼ lb plain chocolate, for decoration

Mix the flour, cocoa, salt, baking powder and brown sugar in a large basin. Crack the eggs, beating the whites stiffly, and put the yolks into a jug with the corn oil, milk and vanilla essence, stirring very thoroughly until they are completely mixed. Make a hollow in the dry ingredients, and pour in the liquid a little at a time, using a wooden spoon, and beating well to make sure that the mix is absolutely smooth. Now fold in the eggwhites, and turn the mixture into a cake tin that has been lined with one unbroken piece of (slightly greased) kitchen foil. Bake in a moderate oven (350 F, Gas mark 4) for $1\frac{1}{4}$ hours. Test with a skewer, and if it is done, take the cake from the oven and allow it to cool – still in its foil-lined tin. Now make a syrup from the granulated sugar and water; bring to the boil and simmer for five minutes, then stir in the rum. Prick the cake in several places with a skewer (but take care you don't puncture the tinfoil as well) and pour the hot syrup over to soak in. Leave this overnight to absorb completely.

Next day, lift out the foil and remove the 'rich, damp cake' (despite what Captain Hook said, it won't hurt you!) and put it on a serving-dish. Whip the cream thickly and cover the top and sides of the cake like a snowball. Finally, grate the chocolate, using the largest holes in the grater to produce thin curls of chocolate, and sprinkle these all over the top of the cream. Leave the cake to chill for at least another hour or two before you serve it.

Bortsch
Steak & Kidney Pie
Apple Snow

BORTSCH

There are many different kinds of bortsch but the characteristic of this famous Russian soup is beetroot and a somewhat sharp taste. The following recipe was given to Meg by the wife of a Russian engineer who was attending an international conference in Birmingham. She told her that in the remote parts of Russia, families make great tubs of this 'meal-in-a-soup' and leave them outside to freeze. Then they hack off what they need during the long cold winter – a sort of home made deep-freeze!

4 *pints of stock*	2 *tablespoons vinegar* ⎫ **or to**
4 *beetroots*	1 *tablespoon sugar* ⎬ *taste*
½ *lb cabbage*	1 *bay leaf*
2 *carrots*	1½ *teaspoons salt*
1 *parsnip*	½ *teaspoon pepper*
3 *stalks of celery*	*a good pinch of dill seed*
1 *large onion*	*sprig of parsley*
3 *tablespoons tomato puree*	⅓ *pint sour cream*
(*or ¼ lb fresh tomatoes*)	¼ *lb boiled ham*
	6 *frankfurter sausages*

The decorative appearance and colour of this soup is all important. The cabbage and onion should be shredded finely and the root vegetables should be first sliced and then cut into neat 'matchsticks'. However, one beetroot should be reserved for later use.

Put all the rest of the vegetables, apart from the cabbage, into a large pan. Cover with about half the stock, the sugar and tomato puree and simmer, stirring occasionally, for fifteen minutes. Now add the cabbage (and a little more stock) and simmer for another 15-20 minutes. Put in all the rest of the stock, a tablespoon of vinegar, salt and pepper, the bay leaf and the dill and cook until the vegetables are done.

Now take the remaining beetroot. Shred it finely on a fine grater, cover with a cupful of stock and a teaspoon of vinegar and simmer for about three minutes. Strain this liquid into the bortsch and add a few slices of ham and sausages.

Add the sour cream, sprinkle with parsley and serve.

STEAK AND KIDNEY PIE

So simple to make – anyone can do it, or so they think! But this recipe has one or two special extras that make all the difference. Of course, when all's said and done, a great deal depends on the pastry; and having 'a light hand with pastry' is one of those unfair gifts like perfect pitch or peaches-and-cream complexion – you've either got it or you ain't. If you're in the latter category, take heart; Mrs Cunningham (who helped out in the kitchen for a while and was a dab hand at pastry) used to claim that it was like being lucky at cards – if you have the knack, you're liable to be unlucky in love! And it certainly seemed to be so in her particular case. Ah, well – you can't have everything.

1½ lb beefsteak	½ pint beefstock
¾ lb calf's kidney	1 bay leaf
2 tablespoons flour	1 teaspoon chopped parsley
salt and pepper	powdered cloves
2 tablespoons butter	½ lb flaky pastry
2 tablespoons cooking oil	1 tablespoon sherry
1 small onion	1 teaspoon Worcester sauce

Soak the prepared kidneys in salted water for an hour or so; then dry them well, slice them and roll in seasoned flour, together with the steak, cut into cubes. Chop the onion and fry in the mixed oil and butter until golden, adding the floured meat and stirring until it is well-browned. Now add the stock, a dash of pepper, the bay leaf, parsley and powdered cloves (half a teaspoon, but adjust according to taste). Put a lid on the pan and simmer until the meat is tender (perhaps an hour).

Now roll out your flaky pastry; transfer the contents of the pan to a pie dish and put on the pastry 'lid'. Bake in the oven at 450 F, Gas mark 8 for ten minutes, then reduce the heat to 375 F, Gas mark 5 until the crust is a golden brown. Before dishing up, cut a slit in the pastry and spoon into it the mixed sherry and Worcester sauce.

APPLE SNOW

There are several old apple trees at the end of the kitchen garden behind the Motel – trees that have been there since the days when Crossroads was a private house, and Meg was married to Charles Richardson, and they had two small children . . . living happy ever after, as she believed. An awful lot has happened since then; but the old trees still produce a crop of apples every year, and every year the chefs try to dream up new ways of using the fruit.

1½ lb cooking apples	4 oz castor sugar
2 parings of lemon rind	3 egg whites
3 tablespoons water	green colouring, if required

Peel, core and slice the apples; then put them in a saucepan with the water and the thin leaves of lemon rind. Simmer gently for about a quarter of an hour, until the apples are cooked. Then remove the lemon rind and stir in the sugar; make a puree by rubbing through a sieve or using a blender. If you want to improve the appearance, add a few drops of green colouring. Let the puree chill thoroughly. Beat the egg whites stiffly, and fold into the puree, then whisk again until the mixture is light and frothy. Serve in individual glasses.

Pot au Feu
Chicken Pie
Queen of Puddings

POT AU FEU

Even the revered Mrs Beeton, or, at least, her editors, got carried away in describing the ingredients of this great French dish. It is *not* a matter of putting every left-over you can lay your hands on into a large pot and simmering away for hours. The right ingredients are important and you will finish up, not with a kind of super stew, but with a delicious clear soup (bouillon) and a boiled meat course (bouilli) which in turn will make a delicious cold salad. This is how it is prepared in the Crossroads kitchen from Mr Lovejoy's original recipe.

2 *lb piece of lean beef*
  (silverside, shoulder or
  top rib)
about 2 *lb knuckle of veal*
  or shin of beef (including
  bone)
chicken giblets, if available
6 *pints of water*
4 *large carrots sliced in*
  quarters

1 *large turnip sliced to size*
  of carrot quarters
4 *leeks washed and halved*
1 *large onion, unpeeled*
2 *sticks celery*
1 *clove*
bouquet garni
salt and pepper

The very best way to prepare this dish is to boil the bones first, removing the scum as it rises and leaving them to simmer for as long as possible (four hours or more). The bone stock is then strained through a wet cloth into a basin and any fat is removed before it is used in the pot-au-feu. However, if time is a factor, tie the meat into a neat shape and put it with the bones, giblets etc, into a large pot. Add the cold water and bring slowly to the boil, removing scum as it rises. When only a white froth appears, add the prepared vegetables, seasonings and herbs. When boiling again,

117

skim, partly cover and simmer very gently for three to four hours, when the meat should be tender.

Dish up drained meat surrounded by vegetables and moistened with a little stock.

Strain stock again, season, and either remove fat with absorbent paper or allow to cool so that fat can be removed in one piece.

CHICKEN PIE

Of course, it's so easy nowadays to buy your chicken pie straight from the grocer's freezer cabinet – but it's true to say that there's something about the flavour of a good home-made pie that can't be matched. This is a recipe which Diane picked up while she was staying on her Uncle Ed's Shropshire small-holding – where there might not be much money to spare, but where she ate as well as she's ever done in her life. (Benny generally went out 'over the tops' to collect the mushrooms, by the way.)

1 *small chicken*	$\frac{3}{4}$ *pint chicken stock*
1 *carrot*	1 *glass dry cider*
1 *onion*	*a sprig of parsley*
$\frac{1}{4}$ *lb mushrooms*	1 *bay leaf, salt and pepper*
1 *tablespoon dripping*	*a little milk*
2 *oz butter*	$\frac{1}{2}$ *lb shortcrust pastry*
$1\frac{1}{2}$ *oz flour*	

Peel the carrot and dice it; peel the onion and chop finely. Wash the mushrooms and cut them into quarters. Heat the dripping in a heavy pan, and brown the carrots, onion and (turning it on all sides) the chicken. Then add the cider, stock and seasonings, put on a lid, and simmer for an hour. Now make the shortcrust pastry and leave it in the fridge (that's always a good tip for pastry making – it improves by being chilled). At the end of the hour, take the chicken out of the pan to drain and cool; pour the stock into a jug, and turn the vegetables into a pie dish. When the chicken is cool

118

enough to be manageable, take off the skin, and then cut all the meat from the bones, dicing it into small pieces. Add these to the vegetables in the pie dish.

Heat half the butter in a small pan and lightly cook the mushrooms for a few minutes, then transfer these to the pie dish as well. Now add the rest of the butter, stir in the flour and cook for a little longer – then blend in the stock, a little at a time, bringing to the boil, and then simmering for a few more minutes. Season, pour over the chicken and vegetables, mixing well. Now roll out the pastry and cover the pie; brush the top with a little milk to glaze; and cook in a hot oven (450 F, Gas mark 8) for about twenty minutes, then reduce the heat to 300 F, Gas mark 1 and continue cooking for another hour. If the pastry gets too brown, cover it with a sheet of foil.

QUEEN OF PUDDINGS

This pudding, Larry Grayson says, is his favourite – of course! It needs careful preparation or it becomes a rather soggy shadow of what it should be.

1 *breakfast cup full of white breadcrumbs*	*a little vanilla flavouring*
4 *eggs (three separated)*	3-4 *tablespoons castor sugar*
raspberry jam	1 *pint milk*

Make a custard from the pint of milk, the whole egg and the yolks of three eggs.

Put ½″ layer of raspberry jam into a pie dish. Add the crumbs and a little vanilla flavouring to the custard and pour over the jam. Leave to stand for half an hour. Bake in moderate oven (375 F, Gas mark 5) until set (30-40 minutes). Whip the whites until stiff adding castor sugar. Spread over pudding, dust with castor sugar or icing sugar and bake, until meringue is set and light golden brown in colour. It is possible to substitute 2 oz of semolina for the breadcrumbs by stirring the semolina together with the eggs into the milk while heating it, until it thickens. Useful to know if you are short of bread.

Gnocchi Alla Piedmontese
Boeuf Bourguignon
Castle Pudding

GNOCCHI ALLA PIEDMONTESE

When Vera wants more than a snack on her canal barge, she sometimes has the following dish which she first came across on holiday in Italy.

1½ lb potatoes	salt and pepper
3 oz flour	3 oz butter
1 whole egg	6 oz grated Parmesan
1 yolk of egg	cheese

Boil or steam potatoes and, while still hot, rub through a sieve, then mix in a bowl with the egg and yolk of egg and season with salt and pepper. Roll into walnut-sized balls then flatten out into the shape of small cylinders. Poach in a wide pan of boiling salted water for 20 minutes. Drain and serve with a rich gravy and grated Parmesan cheese.

A tasty variation of this is Gnocchi al Herbe. Add to the sieved potatoes 3 oz of frozen spinach (cooked, well drained and pureed) and a couple of good pinches of chopped parsley, chives, basil and marjoram.

BOEUF BOURGUIGNON

Quite simply – beef in the Burgundy manner; and when Mr Lovejoy ruled the kitchen, he was rather particular that the red wine used in this recipe should be a Burgundian wine. But that's perhaps being a little too fussy, and any good red wine will do perfectly well. In one respect, Mr Lovejoy was quite right; this is a classic French dish, and in its own way, absolutely unbeatable.

1½ lb topside or skirt of beef	1 clove garlic
4 oz streaky bacon	1-2 tablespoons dripping
1 onion	mixed herbs; including
¼ pint red wine	thyme, parsley and a
2 tablespoons olive oil	bay leaf
½ pint beefstock	salt and pepper
1 tablespoon flour	½ lb button mushrooms

Cut the meat up into small cubes, season with salt, pepper and herbs, and put into a pudding basin; then cover with red wine and olive oil mixed together. Leave to marinate – preferably for several hours.

Cut the bacon up into small pieces; peel and chop the onion. Now melt the dripping in a heavy stewpan and fry the bacon lightly, and then lift it out and keep it till it's needed. Fry the chopped onion until it's golden, and keep this aside as well. Now take the meat from the marinade and fry it quickly, making sure it's brown on all sides; then sprinkle in the flour and stir for a few moments. Then pour the marinade liquid in and bring to the boil; add the beefstock, then the crushed clove of garlic and the bay leaf. Cover the pan, reduce the heat until it is simmering comfortably, and let it cook for two hours.

Wash the mushrooms, and add these to the stewpan and cook for half an hour longer.

CASTLE PUDDING

When Meg, Kitty and Andy were young, Granny Fraser used to give them this pudding – one of their favourites. Naturally it has become a firm favourite with their children as well.

2 eggs	3 oz self-raising flour
3 oz butter	jam
3 oz sugar	

Put the butter and sugar into a basin and beat well together until creamed.

Add the eggs, beating all the time, then the flour. As the mixture should be beaten for ten minutes, use a food mixer if you have one!

A few drops of vanilla may be added after the flour if you wish.

Butter small castle pudding tins and half fill them with the mixture. Bake in hot oven (425-450 F, Gas mark 7-8) for twenty minutes.

Turn out of moulds, arrange on a dish and top each pudding with a spoonful of jam.

French Onion Soup
Lamb Cutlets Shrewsbury
Oranges in Caramel Syrup

FRENCH ONION SOUP

When Bernard Booth was working in Paris he bought his meat from the great French market, Les Halles. Here he would see the market workers restoring their strength with steaming bowls of onion soup, and he often joined them. Here is the recipe for this classic French dish.

1½ *oz butter*	2 *pints boiling beef stock*
1 *tablespoon olive oil*	*salt and pepper to taste*
1 *lb Spanish onions, thinly*	4 *slices French bread*
sliced	*grated cheese*
1-2 *level teaspoons sugar*	

Heat butter and oil in a heavy saucepan. Add onions and stir. Cover and cook slowly over low heat until onions are soft. Sprinkle with sugar and stir over medium heat until the onions are gold in colour.

Add stock and seasonings, cover and simmer for 20 to 30 minutes.

Meanwhile bake the bread in a slow oven until dry and pale brown (about 30 minutes). Sprinkle with olive oil and cover with grated cheese.

Put the bread croutes in a flame-proof tureen. Pour the boiling soup over them, sprinkle with more cheese and put under hot grill until bubbling and rich gold in colour.
Serve at once.

LAMB CUTLETS SHREWSBURY

Avis Warren remarked, the first time she saw Mr Booth preparing this dish: 'I don't know what Shrewsbury's got to do with it – the chef at my last hotel used to cook lamb cutlets the same way, and that was in Droitwich!' Mr Booth tried to explain that 'Shrewsbury' is the name given to this old English recipe which dates back at least 150 years, and the reasons for the name are probably long forgotten – but he might just as well have saved his breath. Avis still referred to it as 'Lamb cutlets Droitwich' – much to the confusion of the customers.

8 lamb cutlets
½ oz dripping
¼ lb button mushrooms
1 level teaspoon flour
¼ pint stock

4 tablespoons redcurrant jelly
2 tablespoons Worcester sauce
1 tablespoon lemon juice
salt and pepper

Cut any excess fat from the cutlets, and fry them on both sides in the hot dripping; then put into an oven dish, sprinkling them with the mushrooms, and keep on one side. Now stir the flour into the hot fat still in the pan, and cook through until the flour browns gently. Meanwhile mix the redcurrant jelly, Worcester sauce and lemon juice in a small saucepan over a low heat, until the jelly is melted; then stir this mixture into the browned flour. Add the stock to make up a rich gravy, season with salt and pepper, and bring to the boil. Now pour over the cutlets and mushrooms; put on a lid and cook in a low oven (325 F, Gas mark 3) for 1½ hours.

ORANGES IN CARAMEL SYRUP

A regular stand-by on the sweet trolley; the chefs take care to keep a deep glass bowl replenished with oranges and syrup at all times. Rich, yet refreshing, it makes a perfect 'grand finale' after any meal.

4 *oranges*	about $\frac{1}{3}$ *pint water*
4 *oz castor sugar*	

Slice the top and bottom from each orange, then pare away all the remaining peel and pith, cutting right down to the fruit. Place the oranges in the serving bowl.

Now for the syrup; put the sugar in a heavy pan over a low heat until it has melted, and keep stirring until it all dissolves and caramelises. Take away from the heat and add about half the water – but be very careful at this stage, as the cold water will bubble and spit violently when it meets the hot caramel. Return to the heat and stir until it blends; add the remaining water, or as much as you need to make up a thin syrup. Let it cool, pour into the bowl of oranges, and leave them to marinate overnight or even longer.

You should keep back half a dozen pieces of thin orange rind and remove all the white pith from these, then shred the peel into matchsticks. Put them in a small saucepan and just cover with cold water; bring to the boil, drain, re-cover with fresh cold water and repeat the process. Then let them simmer for twenty minutes until the peel is soft. Drain, and sprinkle on top of the marinaded oranges in the bowl before serving.

Leek Soup
Steak au Poivre
Bananas en Croute with Lemon Sauce

LEEK SOUP

We've discussed chilled soup for warm weather; here's the other side of the coin – something warming for chilly weather!

1 *lb leeks*	1½ *pints water*
2 *back rashers*	*parsley, bay leaf, herbs and*
1½ *pints chicken stock*	*seasoning to taste*

Wash the leeks carefully, making sure no specks of earth are lurking within those tight layers of green leaves. Now chop them finely, and pop them into a saucepan with all the other ingredients. Let this soup cook very slowly – simmering at the lowest heat for 2½ hours or so. Remove the bay leaf, check the seasoning, and dish up.

STEAK AU POIVRE

There are two classic recipes for peppered steaks; the most famous one involves a creamy pepper sauce which covers the meat entirely. This one is simpler and – because it leaves the flavour and texture of the steak to speak for itself – many English diners seem to prefer it.

4 *good steaks – rump,*	1 *tablespoon finely-chopped*
entrecote, or if you've	*shallots or spring onions*
just won the pools, fillet!	2 *heaped tablespoons of*
3 *oz butter*	*mixed black and white*
2 *dessertspoonsful of olive*	*peppercorns*
oil	¼ *pint good stock*
	3 *tablespoons brandy*

Trim the steaks, removing excess fat and gristle. Take the peppercorns and crush them well; some people use a pestle and mortar for this, but when Avis tried it, she finished up with peppercorns richocheting off the kitchen walls like buckshot. A safer method is to fold the peppercorns into a clean teacloth, folding it over several times, then crush them with a rolling-pin. Now rub the crushed pepper into the steaks, pressing well in on both sides. Cover, and leave for some time – several hours, preferably.

Cook in a mixture of 1 oz of the butter and olive oil until the steaks are browned on each side. Put aside and keep hot. Add another ounce of butter to the pan and cook the chopped onions for a minute or two; then pour in the stock and brandy and cook quickly, stirring in any brown residue from the bottom of the pan. Lastly, stir in the final ounce of butter, then pour this delicious sauce over the hot peppered steaks, and serve.

BANANAS EN CROUTE WITH LEMON SAUCE

When Andy and Ruth went to Jamaica on business for their travel agency, they discovered a whole world of exciting new foods. They had, of course, eaten bananas before; but never like this. They are now regularly on the Crossroads menu.

1 *lb sweet short crust pastry*	**For the sauce:**
1 *banana per head*	2 *lemons*
raisins or sultanas	1 *oz butter*
butter	1 *heaped teaspoon*
brown sugar	*cornflour*
cinnamon	3 *oz demerara sugar*
	water

Roll out pastry and divide into squares of a size suitable for covering a banana. Put ripe banana on the square and sprinkle with raisins and a pinch of cinnamon, a small knob of butter and some brown sugar. Wet edges of pastry, fold over neatly and pinch together. Brush with beaten egg and bake at 375 F, Gas mark 5 for 40 minutes and serve hot with the following sauce.

Finely grate the rind of the lemons. Melt butter in saucepan and add the cornflour, stirring constantly, then add the rind and juice of the lemons. Slowly bring to the boil, still stirring, then add enough water to give the consistency of thin custard. Bring to boil again and cook for a few minutes before serving.

Curried Eggs
Tripe and Onions
Baked Caribbean Bananas

CURRIED EGGS

Something with a tang of the Far East! Nobody seems to remember where this recipe came from, unless Meg's one-time ward, Dr Bruce Richardson, brought it back on one of his leaves from Singapore.

> 4 *hard-boiled eggs, sliced*
> ½ *pint curry sauce (either a*
>   *white sauce cooked with*
>   *curry powder – or else*
>   *you can take the easy*
>   *way out and buy a ready-*
>   *mixed curry sauce)*
> 4 *oz rice*
>
> ½ *teaspoon salt*
> 1 *tablespoon washed*
>   *sultanas*
> 2 *tablespoons mango*
>   *chutney*
> 4 *pineapple rings*
> *sprigs of parsley*

Boil the rice with the salt in ½ pint cold water; stir, lower the heat, and let it simmer for about a quarter of an hour, until the rice is tender. Make up the curry sauce and blend in the sultanas and chutney. Dish up the boiled rice in a ring shape, with the sauce in the middle, and top with slices of egg and pineapple rings, garnishing with a few sprigs of parsley.

BAKED CARIBBEAN BANANAS

Remember Melanie? – the coloured waitress who used to startle unsuspecting guests by addressing her employer cheerily as Aunt Meg (because Meg had known her ever since she was a little girl in a nearby Children's Home, and had become an honorary 'auntie' over the years). Melanie originally hailed from the London area, and when there was talk in political circles of repatriating coloured people to their birthplaces, Melanie used to say she'd be perfectly happy to go back to Walthamstow any time Mr Powell paid her fare.

But being a cockney didn't stop her dreaming now and again about the sunny West Indies – and this Caribbean recipe is one she was particularly fond of.

4 *bananas*	2 *tablespoons rum*
1 *small tin pineapple cubes*	1½ *tablespoons brown sugar*
juice and rind of one	*double cream*
orange	

Grate the orange rind and keep aside for garnishing. Slice the bananas longways and place in a buttered oven dish, with the pineapple cubes. Squeeze the orange and combine the juice with the juice from the pineapples and the rum. Pour this over the fruit, and sprinkle with the brown sugar; then top with a garnish of grated orange rind. Place in the oven uncovered, and cook for half an hour (375 F, Gas mark 5). Serve piping hot, with a generous spoonful of cream for each portion.

TRIPE AND ONIONS

Most people who shudder at the thought of eating tripe and onions have probably never tried it. Anyway it was one of Wilf Harvey's favourite meals and this is how his wife used to cook it.

2 *lb tripe*	1 *oz flour*
cold water	½ *pint milk*
1 *teaspoon salt*	*pepper and paprika*
4 *large onions*	*good pinch of nutmeg*

Buy cleaned tripe. Put in a saucepan, cover with water and bring to the boil. Remove tripe from pan and cut into 2½″ squares. Return to rinsed pan and again cover with cold water. Add salt and bring to the boil. Add sliced onions, cover and simmer until tender (about 2 to 3 hours). Drain the water off. Mix the flour with the milk to a paste. Stirring constantly, add to the tripe and bring to the boil. Simmer for fifteen minutes. Season to taste with salt, pepper and paprika. Serve on a hot dish with mashed or new potatoes.

Grilled Grapefruit
Carbonnades Flamandes
Baked Alaska

GRILLED GRAPEFRUIT
Yes, it does sound a bit odd, doesn't it? – hot grapefruit . . .? But do try it; it really is a new taste sensation. And it has the added bonus of being very, very easy to prepare.

two grapefruits	*sugar*
cinnamon	

Slice the grapefruit in halves, separate the segments carefully, cutting each side of the pithy membranes with a sharp, pointed knife. Sprinkle with cinnamon and sugar and heat through under a moderately hot grill, until the sugar is lightly browned.

CARBONNADES FLAMANDES
This is a traditional Flemish beef stew, cooked in beer, and is every bit as warming and filling as you would expect. Carney, who doesn't altogether approve of what he calls

'them fancy foreign concoctions' tasted this and gave it his seal of approval right away. 'Good enough for the Queen of England herself' was his verdict. 'After all – it's got beer in it, 'en't it? – and what could be more English than that?'

1 *lb steak*	½ *lb onions*
2 *tablespoons flour*	½ *pint beer*
1½ *teaspoons salt*	1 *tablespoon vinegar*
¼ *teaspoon pepper*	½ *teaspoon sugar*
2 *tablespoons dripping*	*mixed herbs*

Cut the steak up into small cubes, coat in a little flour, salt and pepper, then fry in dripping until the meat is well browned. Put the meat in a casserole, and fry the sliced onions in the hot fat. Add the rest of the flour and cook for a few minutes, then pour the beer into the pan and continue stirring until it boils. Pour the whole lot over the meat, adding herbs and sugar; then cook slowly (315 F, Gas mark 2) for two hours or more – as with all stews, the longer they can cook, the better. Stir in the vinegar just before you dish up.

BAKED ALASKA

Sheila Mollison (who used to be Sheila Harvey) is a working wife and mother, and last October, when her small daughter Susan had her third birthday, Sheila invited some neighbouring children around for a special tea-party. She tried to think up some kind of unusual sweet, and asked Meg's advice; with the result that a noisy party of two-, three- and four-year-olds were hushed by the splendour of a very thrilling dessert (which figures on French menus as 'omelette Norvegienne') which they received with rapture and astonishment. Ice-cream out of the oven – it was as good as a conjuring trick!

1 *thin layer of sponge cake as a base (or buy a ready-made flan base)*	3 *egg whites*
	4 *oz castor sugar*
	1 *family brick of ice-cream*
1 *small tin pineapple cubes*	

Make a meringue by whipping the egg whites until they are very stiff. (The traditional test for this is that you should be able to turn the bowl full of stiffly beaten egg white upside down above your head. . . . But Sheila had just got Vera to give her a quick hair-do at the Salon, and didn't care to risk it). Then fold in the sugar, lightly.

Now put the sponge base on an ovenproof dish or sandwich tin, and make a layer of pineapple cubes upon it; then put the ice-cream brick on top of the pineapple. Finally spoon the meringue thickly over the whole lot, making sure that there are no gaps; a protective armour of meringue must enclose the ice-cream completely. Place it in the oven, turned up to maximum temperature, for five to ten minutes. Ideally, it ought to come out looking like a crisp brown loaf. Then bring it straight to the table and serve. Piping hot outside, ice-cold within – it's magic!

Duck Terrine
Roast Turkey with Chestnut Stuffing
Christmas Pudding

DUCK TERRINE

This is an absolutely superb first course; not a smooth pate (like our 'Pate Maison') but a rough, crumbly terrine, with a texture and a flavour that Mr Booth once described as 'irresistibly reminiscent of old-fashioned French farmhouse cooking'.

To start with – have roast duck for dinner the day before! No, it's not a cheap meal, but duck's always something to remember on one of those very special occasions. (And if you serve it in the Crossroads manner, with our rich orange sauce, it'll be even more special.) This terrine is a wonderful way of using up the giblets and all the meat that is left on the carcase. Which is why the recipe starts off:

131

as much left-over duck as you can scrape together! (*together with the liver, heart and gizzard, but remove the bits of skin*)

1 lb lean pork and ½ lb fat pork, minced up and mixed in (*ask your butcher nicely and he'll do this for you*)

2 cloves of garlic, and a generous pinch of mixed herbs

10 juniper berries

1½ tablespoons of brandy and a tin of frozen orange juice concentrate

enough thinly-cut streaky bacon rashers to line the terrine (¾ lb?)

For garnishing:

bay leaves

a couple of slices from an orange

jellied consomme

a tablespoon of sherry

1 teaspoon gelatine powder

First of all, mince your left-over duck pieces and the bird's innards. Mix this with the minced pork, together with the garlic and eight of the juniper berries all crushed up together, and the herbs, brandy, and half a tablespoonful of the frozen orange juice. Add salt and pepper fairly liberally.

Then take the rinds off the bacon and line your terrine (which is an oven-proof earthenware dish like a small shoe-box, with a fitted lid) – covering the bottom and then all four sides. Spoon in the mixture until it's full, then finish it off with a top layer of bacon and pop two bay leaves on top. Put a final layer of buttered greaseproof paper over it all. Put on the lid, and stand the terrine in a roasting-pan that's half full of cold water. Cook it in a pre-heated slow oven (250 F, Gas mark ½) for three hours.

Next take off the lid and remove the greaseproof paper and bay leaves. The mixture will have shrunk in the cooking and be surrounded by a greasy juice, which you must pour away (being careful not to scald your fingers in the process). Now put a heavy weight on top of the terrine (how about a couple of two-pound jamjars full of water, if you haven't got any weights kicking around?) and leave it all for several hours – preferably all night – until it's set firmly into shape. Then slide a hot knife round the sides and carefully turn the terrine out of its dish (run some hot water over the bottom of the dish if it's being stubborn) and set it aside while you wash out the dish and dry it thoroughly. Return the terrine to its dish, and garnish it.

For this, you need a jellied mixture made up of three or four tablespoons of the consomme with the gelatine dissolved in it to make it stiffer; then combine this with the sherry and another half-tablespoon of frozen orange juice. Pour the lot into the dish so that all the cracks round the sides are filled up, then decorate the top with the slices of orange, each with a juniper berry stuck in the middle, and two small bay leaves to make a flower pattern. Finish off with a little more of the jelly to glaze this decoration. Let the terrine chill in the fridge, then serve it in thin slices to your guests. Admittedly it sounds complicated, but it's not really difficult – and it tastes delicious.

ROAST TURKEY – WITH CHESTNUT STUFFING
What else can you have for Christmas dinner except a roast turkey? Well, frankly – almost anything! For a start, many domestic ovens are too small to take one of those monster turkeys, and many people prefer the more delicate flavour of a capon anyway. Some families in Kings Oak have created their own traditions; at the Post Office, Miss Tatum always has boiled silverside with dumplings on Christmas Day, and invites the postmen in to share it. But if you're going to settle for poultry, here is a superb stuffing with all the old-fashioned Dickensian richness. The quantities are for a ten-pound bird – so if yours is smaller, adjust them accordingly.

1½ lb chestnuts	1 tablespoon chopped
3 oz butter	parsley
4 oz breadcrumbs	2 teaspoons salt, ¼ teaspoon
chicken stock	pepper
¾ lb sausage meat	1 chopped rasher of bacon

Shell the chestnuts (the best way is to cut off the pointed tops, then bake in the oven for a quarter of an hour; let them cool, and you'll find the shells and skin will come off quite easily). If you can't be bothered with this, tins of unsweetened chestnut puree are available – and nobody's going to accuse you of cheating, after all.

If you use whole chestnuts, cook them gently in a little stock until they have softened then pass them through a sieve, or put them in the blender. Then mix in all the other ingredients, adding a little more stock if necessary to bind it together.

CHRISTMAS PUDDING

This is a Harvey family recipe; and Stan swears there's no Christmas pud in the world to touch it. But of course that could be because it includes brown ale among the ingredients – so as far as Stan is concerned, it must be all right. Traditionally cooked on 'Stir-up Sunday', several weeks before Christmas (when the church collect begins: 'Stir up, we beseech Thee, the hearts of Thy people') – the pudding is then kept in a cool place and boiled up again on Christmas morning. At the Harveys, every member of the family had to take a turn with the stirring, by the way, and everyone was supposed to make a wish while carrying out this solemn ritual.

1 lb raisins	$\frac{1}{2}$ lb plain flour
1 lb currants	$\frac{1}{4}$ lb breadcrumbs
1 lb sultanas	1 orange
$\frac{3}{4}$ lb mixed dried peel	1 lemon
6 oz sweet almonds	1 teaspoon mixed spice
$\frac{3}{4}$ lb beef suet	4 eggs
6 oz brown sugar	1 wineglass brown ale
1 teaspoon powdered nutmeg	

Chop the dried fruit and peel, almonds and suet, and mix well with the other dry ingredients. Squeeze the juice from the orange and lemon and stir into the beaten eggs, then add to the mixture. Finally add the brown ale and stir again. This will make enough for two big puddings, so divide the mixture into two bowls, covering them with pudding cloths or a kitchen foil top. Simmer gently in boiling water for 4 hours.

At the little house by the canal, one pudding was eaten on Christmas Day, and the other – which always kept perfectly in the larder – was saved for Easter Sunday.

ROAST—AND EIGHT VEG

So much for our fifty-two menus. But before we move on, let's not overlook the fact that for every main course, the kitchen has to provide an accompaniment of vegetables. And if that sounds dull – it shouldn't!

We all take for granted the dear old diehards like carrots and cabbage; 'roast and two veg' has been a bad joke for a long time. But it's not difficult, with a little imagination, to present a traditional dish with something really original and enterprising alongside. That's why we're taking this opportunity to introduce not one or two but *eight* recipes for veg – to give a new sparkle to old favourites.

RATATOUILLE

Now that market gardeners (like Ed Lawton) are providing us with native courgettes and peppers, ratatouille is no longer something you can only meet on holiday in the Mediterranean. People with greenhouses are experimenting with the more difficult aubergines, too; but this is another of those basic recipes that you can improvise, according to what happens to be available.

½ lb tomatoes (or a 15 oz tin of tomatoes)
½ lb courgettes
½ lb peppers (green and red, preferably)
½ lb aubergines
2 medium onions, chopped
a clove of garlic
2 or 3 tablespoons of oil
oregano

Fry the onion and crushed garlic in the oil. Chop the courgettes, peppers and aubergines, and add to the mixture. Cook for about ten minutes on a medium heat. Add the tomatoes and cook for a further ten minutes – longer, if you want a very smooth texture – stirring and shaking the pan frequently. Add salt, pepper and oregano to taste.

CARROTS VICHY

1 *oz butter*	1 *teaspoon sugar*
1 *lb young carrots, sliced*	1 *tablespoon chopped*
½ *teaspoon salt*	*parsley*

Melt the butter in a saucepan and add the other ingredients, except the parsley. Cover and cook very gently until the carrots are tender (about 20 minutes). Sprinkle with parsley and serve.

DUCHESSE POTATOES

Allow ½ lb of potatoes for each person. Peel and boil in salted water until they are soft enough to mash. For each pound of potatoes, add 1 egg yolk, 1 tablespoon of milk, 1 oz of butter, salt, pepper and a pinch of nutmeg. Pipe through a forcing bag in rosettes on to a greased tray and bake in a hot oven (425 F, Gas mark 7) until golden. The mixture can be used to decorate dull dishes, or be piped as a border around Coquille St Jacques, and all children welcome a variation from plain boiled or mashed.

FRENCH-FRIED ONION RINGS

flour	*fine salt*
1 *large onion* (*per person*)	*flour*
sliced into rings	*fat or oil for frying*

Sprinkle the onions with salt and leave for 20 minutes. Drain, sprinkle with flour and fry in hot fat or oil for five minutes. Remove the onions; they will be soft and still white, but don't despair. Re-heat the fat until there is a blue haze over the pan, and fry the onions again until they are crisp and golden.

CUCUMBER AND YOGHURT SALAD

1 medium-sized cucumber
½ onion, finely chopped
1 carton plain yoghurt

salt and freshly-milled
    pepper
1 or 2 teaspoons finely
    chopped parsley or mint

Peel the cucumber and cut in half lengthwise. Remove the centre seeds and dice the flesh. Put in a bowl with the chopped onion, then add the yoghurt, seasoning and the mint or parsley. Mix well. This is excellent as an accompaniment to grilled chops, steak or curry.

CHICORY AND ONION SALAD

4 heads of chicory
1 small bunch of spring
    onions
1 tablespoon of white wine
    vinegar

3 tablespoons olive oil
1 teaspoon made mustard
1 teaspoon castor sugar
salt and pepper

Cut off the base of the chicory and any tough outer leaves. Clean the spring onions and cut off leaves to within half an inch of the white bulbs. Cut chicory and onions into thin slices. Combine the oil, vinegar, mustard, sugar and seasoning. Toss the salad in this dressing and serve. It's specially good as a side-dish with chicken.

PEAS – FRENCH STYLE

2 lbs peas (or 1 lb frozen
    peas)
1 oz butter
4 or 5 shallots or 10 spring
    onions
½ teaspoon salt

4 or 5 outside leaves of
    lettuce
2 rashers of bacon,
    chopped
2 or 3 tablespoons of water
a pinch of pepper

Line the bottom of a saucepan with the lettuce leaves. Put in all the ingredients, and finish with another layer of lettuce; then cook gently until the peas are tender. Check to see that there is enough water to keep the pan from burning; replenish if necessary, but do not make too much liquid.

RED CABBAGE

1 *oz dripping*	2 *tablespoons vinegar*
1 *lb red cabbage, shredded*	1 *teaspoon salt, and a pinch*
1 *large onion, sliced*	*of pepper*
1 *large apple, sliced*	1 *tablespoon brown sugar*
2 *tablespoons beefstock or*	
water	

Melt the dripping in a saucepan and add all the other ingredients. Cover and simmer for ¾ hour, until the cabbage is tender. Stir and shake frequently, so that the mixture does not stick to the pan, but there should be hardly any liquid left at the end of cooking. This vegetable freezes perfectly, and is very good served with pork, sausages or gammon.

HOME COOKING

So much for the Motel dining-room, with its many satisfied customers (most of the time) and its prompt, efficient waitresses (some of the time!). But the Crossroads Motel isn't just an impersonal catering organisation—far from it.

Meg has always maintained that the success of the Motel is based on friendliness; however many guests come and go through the swinging glass doors, she insists that the original family atmosphere must be retained. It's certainly true that all the regulars who return again and again to Kings Oak feel a certain personal link with the place and the people.

First and foremost, the Crossroads Motel *is* a family affair; not only the genuine family (now in its third generation, thanks to Sarah-Jane Harvey) but, in a deeper sense, people like David and Vera and Tish are just as much a part of the family circle. Even when some of them go away, as Diane has had to do from time to time, they always come back, and their return is always very much a homecoming.

That is why, at this point, it is important to turn away from the professional techniques of the restaurant and concentrate instead on the meals that are prepared for that family – behind the scenes, so to speak; snacks and sweets and little extras that never find their way on to any menu, but which are the essence of 'home cooking'.

For a start, there's the staff room, over in the kitchen wing; because the staff too must be fed – whether it's a breakfast snack when they arrive for work first thing in the morning, or a late supper to send them off happily last thing at night. Often the main dishes may come from the same bill of fare which they have been serving to the guests – but sometimes they might prefer something lighter, and then Shughie McFee will probably turn to and produce something like –

KEDGEREE

8 *oz cooked, flaked, smoked haddock*	2 *tablespoons cream*
2 *oz butter*	1 *small onion*
8 *oz boiled rice*	*lemon juice*
2 *hard-boiled eggs*	*seasoning*
	chopped parsley to garnish

(If you want to know how to cook the haddock, see David Hunter's recipe for scrambled eggs on the next page – but remember that you will need about 8 oz of fish *after* it has been skinned, boned and flaked – which means starting with about ¾ lb of smoked haddock.)

Chop the onion and cook very gently in butter; then stir in the cooked rice and the flaked fish. Add the cream to moisten the mixture and heat through; then the hard-boiled eggs, coarsely chopped into crumbs. Season with salt and pepper, sprinkle with parsley and serve.

Meg once experimented by preparing a kedgeree without cream and chilling it in the fridge, then stirring in the cream when it was cold. It made a sensational picnic dish for an outdoor party!

Or, instead, Mr Booth might fall back on that classic French dish which makes an ideal light snack, with a little salad on the side – a kind of egg-and-cheese flan, known by the more imposing title –

QUICHE LORRAINE

You will find all kinds of occasions when a quiche will be useful; for parties and picnics, as a snack in the middle of the day, or more elaborately presented in the evening. You'll often find it served in French restaurants as an *hors d'oeuvre*, and you can introduce it as part of a packed meal. This is a basic recipe; you will soon find other variations for the filling yourself.

4 oz short crust pastry
½ oz butter
1 medium onion, chopped
3 oz lean bacon, chopped
2 eggs

3 oz grated cheese
½ pint milk
3 tablespoons double cream
salt and pepper

Line a sandwich tin with the pastry. Melt the butter and fry the onion until soft, add the bacon and cook through. Beat the eggs and add the grated cheese, milk and cream. Season with salt and pepper, and stir in the bacon and onion mixture. When it has blended, pour it into the pastry-lined tin.

Bake in the centre of a hot oven (400 F, Gas mark 6) for 25 minutes. Reduce the heat to 375 F, Gas mark 5 and cook for a further ten minutes. Suggested additions are: slices of tomato, mushrooms, chopped red or green peppers, chopped leek instead of the onion – but the possibilities are almost never-ending.

David Hunter has lived alone for long stretches of time; at Lake Cottage, after Rosemary left him; and at the cottage he bought and converted, and later sold to Meg and Hugh. Recently, he has been living at the Motel, but sometimes he may stay late in the office, catching up on paperwork, and that's where he can be found after the staff have gone, foraging in the empty kitchen and making a midnight snack for himself. Like all good hoteliers, David has been well trained in kitchen skills and is no mean cook himself; but the supper dish he returns to time and again is simple, straightforward – and quick –

DAVID HUNTER'S SCRAMBLED EGGS

4 eggs
1 carton cream
½ lb smoked haddock
2 oz butter

2 tablespoons grated cheese
salt and pepper
4 slices of toast

143

Poach the haddock in enough milk to cover it for approximately ten minutes, until the flesh is firm and comes away in flakes. Now skin it and remove all the bones – a fiddly job, but terribly important! Flake the fish into a saucepan and heat over a low flame with one ounce of the butter – then stir in most of the carton of cream. Put this aside to keep hot while you beat the eggs with the rest of the cream (about a tablespoonful) and season.

Cook your scrambled eggs in the usual way, and as they begin to set, stir in half the grated cheese; then add the creamed haddock and mix well. Butter the slices of toast, spoon a quarter of the mixture on to each slice, and sprinkle with the remaining grated cheese; then pop under the grill for a few moments – and serve!

Someone else who has lived alone for a time is Mrs Hope – known to one and all as 'Tish' (because her real name, Venetia, is, she admits herself, too much of a mouthful for anybody). Now Tish and Ted are reunited, and their friends are keeping their fingers crossed for this happy state of affairs to continue. But there were times when Tish was on her own, and particularly after son and daughter-in-law (Peter and Marilyn) went out to live and work in Africa, she felt horribly lonely. That's why she welcomed any friends who might drop in at the little flat above the antique shop in the village – and why she became skilful at whipping up meals for unexpected guests at very short notice.

Main courses weren't too much of a problem; there's always the good old omelette, with a filling of bacon or tomato or mushroom – or whatever she happened to have by her – but the dessert was a little more difficult. Then one day Tish hit on this solution to the problem, and from that moment on she always kept a tin of green figs in the larder in case of emergencies – and the remains of a bottle of Pernod in the sideboard. To quote Tish herself: 'Well, every time I've nipped over the channel for a quick holiday in

France, I've brought back a bottle of Pernod because it's so much cheaper out there – and then I never get around to finishing it afterwards; it doesn't seem the same in England, somehow. So there's generally one bottle at the back of the shelf, gathering dust . . . and this is a gorgeous way of using it up. Not only that, but my friends get frightfully impressed by this very glamorous – and very *easy* – recipe!

GREEN FIGS IN PERNOD

1 *tin of green figs*   *Pernod* (*you won't need very*
double cream   *much*

Divide the figs up among your guests – roughly three or four per person; and split the syrup from the tin between them as well. Then add three teaspoons of Pernod for each helping, plus a generous dollop (say a tablespoon) of cream on top. It couldn't be more simple – or more sophisticated.

Everyone has a favourite supper snack. Stan Harvey remembers when he was a lad, coming home from school on a cold winter afternoon to find that his Mum had made a special treat for him and Sheila and (before he went off to sea) elder brother Len. . . . It's still a favourite with Stan now, and sometimes Jill makes it for him after a long day at the garage.

BAKED POTATOES WITH GRATED CHEESE
These are delicious at any time, but perhaps most successful at Hallowe'en and bonfire parties. Don't be afraid to ask your greengrocer to pick out big potatoes for baking. Allow one large potato and 2 oz of cheese for each person; salt and pepper and a knob of butter; parsley, and slices of tomato.
Bake the potatoes in the oven; either for 1 hour at 380 F, Gas mark 5, or if you are cooking a casserole at the same time, put them in the bottom of the oven for several hours on a lower heat. When cooked, cut the potatoes in half and

mash them inside their skins with salt, pepper and butter.
Put the grated cheese on top, and cook under the grill until
the cheese bubbles. Decorate with slices of tomato and
parsley.

At weekends, Meg and David take it in turns to stay on duty
at the Motel; and when Meg has a weekend off she likes to
spend it at the cottage, taking things easy. So when it comes
to mealtimes, she prefers to fall back on recipes that don't
require a lot of preparation. Things like –

STUFFED GREEN PEPPERS
These are particularly good made with cooked minced pork,
which is sometimes difficult to use up because it doesn't
combine very well with many of the usual 'left-over' recipes.
But you can use any kind of cooked meat or ham.

2 *large or 4 small peppers*	1 *egg*
1 *small onion, chopped*	1 *tablespoon chopped*
1 *oz fat or 1 tablespoon*	*parsley*
cooking oil	*salt and pepper*
1½ *oz boiled rice or* ⅓ *cup*	½ *pint white sauce with*
breadcrumbs	1 *tablespoon of tomato*
4 *oz minced meat or ham*	*puree stirred in*

Cut the peppers in half and scrape out seeds and membranes.
Fry the onion in the fat, and add the meat, rice, egg, salt,
pepper and parsley. Fill the peppers with this mixture and
place them in a baking dish. Pour over the sauce and cook at
350 F, Gas mark 4, until tender (about 45 minutes).

If the family are coming over for the day, Meg has to think
up a meal on a slightly bigger scale; perhaps a plain roast
joint or a chicken – but nowadays meat comes expensive if
you're feeding a large family, and anyway it soon gets
monotonous if you keep returning to roast-and-two-veg
every Sunday. A much cheaper alternative, and one which

seems to be popular with all three generations of the family,
is –

SPAGHETTI BOLOGNAISE

One pound of spaghetti will feed six normal appetites. Boil
in one gallon of salted water for twelve to fifteen minutes.
Drain in a colander, pouring boiling water over it to separate
the pieces.

Two ounces of minced meat per person is sufficient. Fry it
in a little oil, stirring all the time. Now make a ratatouille
(following the recipe on page 137) – or better still, thaw a
portion of ratatouille that you have made in advance and
kept in the freezer for just such an occasion! Add the
ratatouille to the mince, and heat through. Serve on top of
the spaghetti – and sprinkle with a little grated cheese.

Having talked about an economical Sunday lunch, let's go
to the other extreme. Every now and again Meg lashes out
and orders a duckling from a nearby farm. Roast duck is
always a treat – but even more so when it's accompanied by
Meg's very own –

ORANGE SAUCE

Meg first concocted this when she was a young bride, horribly
nervous of giving dinner parties; she found that sauces made
when suffering from nerves very often went lumpy! But after
trial and error, she still claims that this one is foolproof.

2 *heaped teaspoons of gravy*
mix
½ *pint of stock or water*
3 *tablespoons of red wine*

1 *generous teaspoon of*
frozen concentrated
orange juice
1 *orange – separated into*
segments and skinned

Blend the gravy mix and water or stock, and boil for one
minute. Add the wine and orange juice and bring to the boil
again. Put in the orange segments, and cook until they are
heated through: serve steaming hot!

147

Returning to the Motel – it's quite obvious that one way of feeding the kitchen staff must inevitably be by using up leftovers. On an earlier page, we've already dealt with Shepherds Pie (because the Motel's version is so excellent that it merits a place on the restaurant menu) but another good old standby is the invaluable though unloved fishcake. Now and then the Chefs tried putting these fishcakes on the menu as well, but diners seemed to be prejudiced against them, and the experiment was a failure. It's very sad – because if the guests did but know, these are no ordinary fishcakes! . . . They are in fact very popular in the staffroom, where they are known respectfully as –

MR LOVEJOY'S LUXURY FISHCAKES

(At the Motel, these are always made in large batches, and this recipe will make up sixteen fishcakes – enough for eight hungry people! But they freeze perfectly, if you have more than you need; or of course you can cut down the quantities.)

2½ lb smoked haddock	1 tablespoon lemon juice
6 tomatoes	3 oz grated cheese
3 oz flour	2 eggs
6 oz mushrooms	½ lb fresh white
3 oz butter	breadcrumbs
¾ pint milk	seasoning

Wash and slice the mushrooms; skin and puree the tomatoes. Simmer the haddock in the milk for ten minutes; then take out the fish and strain the juice and milk into a jug. Skin, bone and flake the fish carefully. Saute the mushrooms in butter for about five minutes, together with the lemon juice. Now remove the mushrooms and sprinkle the flour into the melted butter and cook for four minutes, stirring thoroughly. Blend in the milk and juices, making a smooth mixture; bring to the boil and simmer for a further four minutes. Take away from the heat and stir in the cheese, pureed tomatoes, mushrooms and flaked fish. Add salt and pepper to season.

Mix well, and put to cool in the fridge until it is firm. Meanwhile flour a pastry board, whisk the eggs, and get the breadcrumbs ready. When the mixture is firm, divide into sixteen portions and shape into fishcakes on the floured board; then dip in egg and breadcrumbs. Fry lightly on each side until cooked through and golden brown.

Naturally, the Motel gets through an enormous amount of bread every day, and so they put in a standing order with the Kings Oak bakery. But now and then, on special occasions, Mrs Rawlings liked to bake her own loaves. Avis and Jane watched the first few times with awed respect; breadmaking seems to be an almost mystical craft. But eventually Jane got bold enough to try her hand at it – and this encouraged Avis to have a go. Now they both agree that, if you follow the rules carefully, there's really nothing very difficult about –

MAKING BREAD

Baking must be one of the most satisfying smells in the world. It fills the whole house with a feeling of well-being. If you want to change a bad mood into a good one (said Mrs Rawlings) – bake a batch of bread. But you must be prepared to spend some time on it; it can't be hurried.

WHITE BREAD

1½ lb strong plain flour	¾ pint water (warm)
1 teaspoon salt	½ oz lard
½ oz dried yeast	teaspoon of sugar

The strong plain flour and dried yeast are sold in most health food shops and supermarkets. The first thing to remember about bread is to keep all the ingredients gently warm. Grease the tins you are going to use (this recipe is for one large, or two small loaves) and pop them into an airing

149

cupboard or the plate warming part of an oven until you need them. Add the salt to the flour and find a warm spot for it. Melt the lard, add it to the water, yeast, and teaspoon of sugar and stir with a fork. Cover with a cloth and wait for ten to twenty minutes until the mixture is frothy. Stir in the flour and salt and mix until you feel the dough beginning to form, then turn it out on to a floured board and knead. If you are angry kneading is very satisfying. You can press and bang, and knuckle the dough as if it were the thing that is getting on your nerves for ten minutes or so, until you are left with a rubbery ball. Put it into the bowl (which you have kept warm) and place it in a large plastic bag, and leave it in – you guessed – a WARM place to double its size. This can take about an hour. Then ten more minutes of that aggressive kneading, and the dough is ready to be shaped into a loaf or loaves. It should come roughly half way up the greased tin. Use a plastic bag to cover it – you are aiming at a hot damp atmosphere – and wait the half hour or so it will take to rise to the top of the tin. Preheat the oven to 450 F, Gas mark 8 and bake for fifteen minutes, reducing the heat to 380 F, Gas mark 5 for a further 30 minutes or until cooked. You will know when that is by giving the loaf a sharp tap with the knuckles on the bottom. If it is hollow sounding your bread is ready to put on a wire rack to cool. Bread keeps very well in the deep freeze. It takes about 4 hours to thaw at room temperature.

WHOLEMEAL BREAD
– follows the same steps as white bread but you use wholemeal flour; treacle, brown sugar, or molasses, instead of white sugar; and 1 oz of lard instead of $\frac{1}{2}$ oz. Wholemeal bread will be more reluctant to rise than the white variety.

ROLLS
At the point when you shape the bread, cut the dough into sections and roll them into balls with the palm of the hand.

Place on a baking sheet, allowing room for them to double in size, putting baking sheet and all into a plastic bag until they have done this. Cook for about ten minutes at 450 F, Gas mark 8.

Some Irish visitors stayed at the Motel recently, on their first-ever visit to England, and they seemed mildly surprised to find that, at teatime, only one kind of bread was available. Mr Booth enquired what else they were expecting, and learned that in Southern Ireland it's customary to serve slices of soda bread as well as the ordinary yeast-risen loaf.

Intrigued by this, he went into a huddle with Mrs Rawlings, and between them they came up with this recipe, which does not need any yeast; their own version of –

IRISH SODA BREAD

1 *lb plain strong flour*
½ *level teaspoon bicarbonate of soda*
1 *level teaspoon salt*

½ *pint sour milk; or fresh milk with 2 teaspoons of lemon juice mixed into it*

Sieve the flour, salt and bicarbonate of soda into your mixing bowl. Make a hollow in the centre and pour in the milk. Mix with a fork, then turn out on to a board and knead lightly. Turn the dough with the smooth side uppermost and put it on a lightly floured baking tray. Score the dough with two cuts from a sharp knife to mark it with a cross; almost, but not quite, dividing it into four quarters. Put in the oven, on the top rack, and bake for half an hour at 425 F, Gas mark 7 until it is done. Place on a wire tray to cool.

Another type of dough is the kind used in making buns and baps; and this is very much in demand over Easter weekend each year, when the Motel makes hot cross buns to be eaten by staff and guests alike. Sandy says he can remember his mother baking her own hot cross buns when he was very

151

young, and even now he gets nostalgic at the spicy warm smell of newly-made –

HOT CROSS BUNS

Hot Cross Buns became a speciality for Good Friday breakfast in the eighteenth century. The commercial product is stodgy and too yellow in colour, starved of currants and peel. Your own will not only be a revelation to taste, but they will be much cheaper than anything you can buy going by the name. This recipe will make 18 buns.

1 lb strong plain flour
¼ teaspoon salt
1 oz fresh yeast (or ½ oz dried yeast)
2 oz castor sugar
4 oz milk
3 oz butter
1 level teaspoon each cinnamon, nutmeg, mixed spices

½ teaspoon mace
3 oz each raisins, candied peel
2 oz almond paste or short crust pastry
1 beaten egg

Bun wash:
2 oz sugar
2½ oz water

Sift flour, salt and spices into a large warm mixing bowl. Put the yeast, a heaped teaspoon of sugar and ¼ lb flour into a pudding basin. Pour the milk into a measuring jug and make up to 8 oz with boiling water from the kettle. With a wooden spoon mix the liquid into the flour, sugar and yeast, as smoothly as possible. Put aside to rise and froth up (about 15 minutes). You can use this time to mix the rest of the sugar and flour and rub in the butter. Form a well in the centre and pour in the yeasty mixture when it is ready. Mix to a dough with a wooden spoon. Turn it out on to a floury surface and knead for 10 minutes, until you have achieved a slightly rubbery texture. If the mixture is too sticky, add more flour until you can handle it easily, and can make it into a ball.

Place the dough into a clean bowl, cover with a damp cloth

or plastic bag and leave to rise in a warm place until it doubles in size – about 1 hour.

Break down the risen dough, kneading in the raisins and peel. Roll the dough into a long sausage shape on the floured surface and cut into 18 equal pieces. Shape into round buns and place them on baking sheets lined with foil leaving room between for the buns to expand. Roll out the almond paste or pastry, and cut into thin strips. Brush the buns with the beaten egg and lay two strips on each bun to form a cross. Cover and leave to prove for 15-30 minutes. Bake at 450 F, Gas mark 8 for 10-15 minutes until nicely browned. While they are cooking boil the sugar and water together until syrupy. Brush over the buns while they are hot. You can keep the buns in a freezer, or in a tin. To reheat give them 10 minutes in a moderate oven at 350 F, Gas mark 4.

Talking of bread reminds us of sandwiches – and for a lot of hints on sandwiches, turn on a few pages to the chapter on Picnics and Packed Lunches . . . and see how humble bread-and-butter comes into its own!

But there is one variety of sandwich that's far from humble; Meg's nephew Brian Jarvis introduced it to the Motel after his long working trip to Scandinavia – the famous open sandwich or –

SMORGASBORD

First, the base – and traditionally this should be a slice of black bread or pumpernickel. But some people find this too strong a flavour, so you might prefer a slice of white bread (with the crust removed). Butter the bread generously, and then place a lettuce-leaf – roughly the same size and shape – on top.

On this platform you can build a wonderful variety of flavours; here are just a few to start you off, and then you can invent some for yourself.

★A slice of ham rolled round (like a dunce's cap on its side) and filled with a spoonful of Russian salad, and garnished with two slices of cucumber and one of tomato.

★A slice of smoked pork loin from the delicatessen, carrying a spoonful of cold scrambled egg with a dash of pickle.

★A slice of pork luncheon meat, topped with a teaspoon of horseradish cream and a prune (with stone taken out).

★Three overlapping slices of processed cheese, alternating with slices of tomato and beetroot peeping out between them.

★Slices of hard-boiled egg, covered with a spoonful of mayonnaise and a teaspoonful of mock caviare to crown it.

★A slice of liver pate, carrying a very crisply grilled (cold) rasher of bacon, and a slice of cucumber.

★A slice of tongue, with shredded green pepper and onion rings.

★Small slices of salami, topped with watercress and a radish rose. You make these by cutting the radish downward in strips from the top towards the stalk; then drop the radish in ice-cold water and the red strips will curl back outward like petals, displaying the white 'rosebud' inside.

★Two slices of Danish blue cheese with two black grapes (seeded) and half a walnut.

★Pieces of marinaded herrings with a wedge of tomato and a lemon twist. You can make lemon, orange or cucumber twists very simply. Take a single slice of any of these, and make a cut from the centre to the outside edge, like the radius of a geometric circle. Now twist the two cut halves in opposite directions; the result is rather like a ballet-dancer doing the splits, and will look very decorative on top of an open sandwich.

As you see, there's no end to the variety of smorgasbord; but be warned – they're more filling than they look, and most people find they can't eat more than two at a sitting.

Perhaps, if the Scandinavian smorgasbord has a distant cousin in Italy, it must be the pizza. Again, it's a kind of open sandwich, though the base isn't a slice of bread but a crisp crusty dough, and the filling has all the rich flavour of the sunny Mediterranean. But it's surprising how this Continental snack is catching on in England; Pizza Parlours are springing up all over the place, and Mr Booth often has to bow to special requests, roll up his sleeves, and make another tray of ever-popular –

PIZZA

Liking pizza is almost as universal as the taste for baked beans. Gear the filling to the palate of your family and you cannot go wrong.

1 *oz fresh, or* ½ *oz dried yeast*	1 *dessertspoon oregano*
	1 *teaspoon salt*
1 *teaspoon sugar*	8 *oz white flour* (*plain*)
¼ *pint warm water*	5 *tablespoons of oil*

Dissolve the yeast and sugar in the warm water. Leave in a warm place for ten minutes or so to froth up. Sieve the flour and salt into a bowl, and make a hole in the centre. When the yeast mixture is ready pour it into the hole, with the oil. Knead for ten minutes until the dough is elastic. If you find it at all sticky, add more flour. Cover with a damp cloth, or place in a plastic bag, and leave to rise for one hour, until it is doubled in size. Roll and pull to cover a baking sheet. Then puree some tomatoes, or use a tin of tomatoes with two or three teaspoons of tomato paste. Spread a little oil – just enough to moisten the dough – and place the tomatoes on it. Onions, fried; minced ham; slices of, or grated, cheese; anchovies; chopped peppers; olives; salami; mushrooms; these are some of the ingredients you can use for a filling. Crushed garlic gives the authentic Italian touch. Cook in a hot oven (425 F, Gas mark 7) for 25 minutes until the mixture is bubbling and the dough cooked.

155

Well, we've talked about bread in its various forms, and after the bread (or so Jill was told by Granny Fraser when she was a 'wee bit of a bairn') good children get cake. Perhaps tea, as a meal, isn't quite the occasion it used to be. As our habits get more continental, we're beginning to abandon the ritual four o'clock tea with scones, sandwiches, pots of jam, and a variety of home-made cakes. Nevertheless, most of the Motel staff break off for a quick cuppa sometime at the end of the afternoon – and when they do, they often look round hopefully for a little something to go with it. If the chefs have been having a baking day, they're in luck. Glenda's favourite is this recipe for –

CHOCOLATE LAYER CAKE

For the cake:
3 *oz self-raising flour*
4 *oz plain chocolate*
3 *oz castor sugar*
2 *eggs*
1 *oz ground rice*
4 *oz butter*
2 *teaspoons of vanilla essence*

For the filling:
4 *oz butter*
8 *oz icing sugar*
1½ *oz plain chocolate*
2 *tablespoons of warm milk*

Line a 6″ cake tin with foil, slightly greased. Mix the flour and ground rice. Melt the chocolate in a basin over a small saucepan of hot water. Cream together the butter, sugar and vanilla essence; add the melted chocolate (which should have almost cooled by now) and mix lightly. Beat in the two eggs, one at a time. Fold in the flour and rice, fill the cake tin and bake on the upper oven rack (350 F, Gas mark 4) for an hour and a quarter. (But test it after an hour – your oven may be hotter than the one in the Crossroads kitchen.) Remove from the tin and leave to cool on a wire tray. Then slice across twice, cutting the cake into equal horizontal thirds. Fill and top with chocolate butter icing.

Cream the butter and sugar together, adding the melted chocolate (melted as above, over a pan of hot water) and then the milk, a little at a time, until the right consistency is reached. This should make enough for two layers of filling and a topping for the cake.

Carney prefers something a little less rich; and he fell for this recipe the first time Mrs Rawlings tried it out. Later, thanks to Mrs Witton's well-meant interference, Carney got the impression that the little gifts Mrs Rawlings was making to him (like this special cider cake, or a mug of hot soup on a cold and frosty morning) were tokens of affection. He actually began to suspect that the dear lady was setting her cap at him – as an eligible, if somewhat elderly, bachelor. And all because she knew he had a sweet tooth, and was partial to a slice of –

CIDER CAKE

½ lb plain flour	1 teaspoon baking powder
1 teaspoon grated nutmeg	5 oz sugar
pinch of salt	2 eggs
5 oz butter	¼ pint strong dry cider

Sift the flour, nutmeg, baking powder and salt together. Cream the butter with the sugar until it's light and fluffy, then beat in the eggs. Turn half the dry flour mixture into the butter mixture, and beat well, then add half the cider. Mix, then add the rest of the flour and cider.

Line a shallow cake tin with foil, grease it lightly, and turn the cake mixture into this. Bake for 45 minutes (350 F, Gas mark 4). Remove from the tin in its foil and leave to cool on a wire tray, then carefully peel off the foil. It tastes good on the first day, but better still after being kept overnight – and served in slices, buttered just as you would a loaf.

Sandy's favourite cake is something far less English, and it first appeared at the Motel when Cynthia Cunningham introduced this recipe – though it is, in its own way, equally traditional. When you make it yourself, be sure to let it cool very slowly indeed, otherwise the beautiful smooth brown top may crack and split open. When it is quite cool, you can chill it a little more in the fridge, and it will taste even better; Sandy swears that this is the perfect way to make –

CHEESECAKE

1 *oz butter*	4 *oz castor sugar*
6 *digestive biscuits*	3 *eggs*
8 *oz carton cottage cheese*	1 *oz cornflour*
8 *oz fresh cream cheese or*	½ *teaspoon vanilla essence*
full fat soft cheese	1 *carton soured cream*

Make the bottom of the cake by crushing the biscuits (using a teacloth and a rolling-pin) and mixing with the melted butter. Spoon this mixture into a greased 8″ cake tin – preferably the kind with a removable base that slides up and out.

Now rub the cottage cheese through a sieve into a basin; add the cream cheese and beat. Then introduce the sugar and beat again. Separate the eggs, beating the yolks only into the cheese mixture, together with the vanilla. Sift cornflour on to the surface and fold in lightly, then add the sour cream. Now beat the whites of the eggs stiffly, and fold these in as well. Turn the entire mixture into the cake tin and bake in a slow oven (300 F, Gas mark 2) for 1½ hours. If you can manage it, leave the cake in the oven after you've turned out the heat, until it is quite cold.

Finally, and most traditional of all – how can we leave the subject of cake-making without giving the Crossroads recipe for something that comes but once a year? . . . Yes, you've guessed it, a real old-fashioned –

CHRISTMAS CAKE

12 *oz plain flour*	4 *eggs*
1 *pinch salt*	4 *tablespoons milk – or*
1 *teaspoon powdered*	*brandy if you're feeling*
cinnamon	*reckless!*
1 *teaspoon mixed spice*	*finely grated rinds of* 1
4 *oz chopped candied peel*	*lemon and* 1 *orange*
4 *oz halved glace cherries*	8 *oz butter*
1 *lb currants*	8 *oz dark brown sugar*
½ *lb sultanas*	1 *tablespoon golden syrup*
½ *lb seedless raisins*	

Sift together the flour, salt, cinnamon and spice. Mix the peel, fruit and cherries. Beat the eggs into the milk (or brandy). Cream the butter with the grated orange and lemon, and the syrup. Gradually beat the egg mixture into this, then the dry ingredients. Last of all, stir in the fruit.

Line a large cake tin with foil; grease it lightly and put in the mixture, smoothing it flat. Put it in the centre of the oven to bake (325 F, Gas mark 3) for 1½ hours, then lower the heat to 275 F, Gas mark 1 for a further 1½ or 2 hours, testing with a skewer to make sure it's cooked all the way through. When it is cool, you can ice and decorate it in any way you like; and you can make this cake (like the Christmas pudding) well in advance of the festive season, because it keeps very well indeed in an airtight tin.

Meg always insists on making the Crossroads cake herself; but then she admits that she's a sucker for Christmas – 'Always was and always will be,' she says.

She loves everything about it, from buying the presents and wrapping them, to hiding them safely and later on bringing them out to put under the tree. Now Sarah-Jane is old enough to know what it's all about, Meg has even more fun; last year she produced a gold paper cone full of special home-made sweets to go into that bulging stocking at the end of the cot. And this is Meg's recipe for Sarah-Jane's –

CHOCOLATE FUDGE

1 *lb granulated sugar*	5 *oz butter*
¼ *pint milk*	4 *oz plain chocolate*
½ *teaspoon vanilla essence*	2 *oz honey*

Grease a flat oven-tin (about 6″ square) and then put all the ingredients (except the vanilla essence) into a heavy sauce-pan. Stir over a gentle heat until the sugar has dissolved, bring to the boil, and cook until it reaches what is known as the 'soft-ball' stage – so called because when you drop a tea-spoonful of the mixture into a cup of cold water, it forms a small, firm ball.

Remove from the heat; allow to cool for five minutes, stir in the vanilla essence, and then beat the mixture until it is thick and creamy. Pour into the tin, mark into squares, and when it is quite cold, cut into cubes.

At the stage when you add the vanilla, you could also put in some nuts and raisins, or chopped dates, or chopped marshmallow if you like – it's all according to taste!

If Christmas Day is a family affair, Boxing Day is a different kind of celebration, because that's when the Motel staff hold their own Christmas party. At the party, Meg helps to serve the food and David takes over the role of barman. Particularly successful last year was a fruit cup that he concocted – there were vast bowls of it made up in reserve, and somehow every drop disappeared by the end of the party. This is David's recipe for –

PARTY PUNCH

2 *bottles dry table cider*	*thinly-cut twists of lemon*
2 *bottles dry white wine*	*peel*
1 *siphon soda-water*	2 *apples*
2 *wine-glasses of brandy*	2 *bananas*
2 *wine-glasses of sherry*	

Chill the cider and wine, and steep the lemon peel in the sherry for an hour before you need it. Then pour the whole lot into a punchbowl (or a very large pastry bowl will do just as well) and decorate with thin slices of apple and banana.

One word in your ear – it's more potent than it appears to be . . . so beware!

Before we leave this chapter on home-made family fare, perhaps we should let Mrs Rawlings have her say. After all, she did come to the Motel as a qualified pastry cook, first and foremost, and as her own contribution, here are a few wise words on pastry making and baking.

SHORT CRUST PASTRY

8 *oz flour*	*a generous pinch of salt*
2 *oz butter*	*about 2 tablespoons of cold*
2 *oz margarine*	*water*

Sift the flour and salt into the bowl, then add small pieces of the fats and rub in with the tips of your fingers until the mixture looks like fine breadcrumbs. Now mix with a knife or kitchen spatula, adding the cold water a few drops at a time until the dough is firm enough to roll out. Flour your pastryboard and rolling-pin lightly, and roll the pastry, lifting and turning it to keep it light and well-aired. Of course the cooking times will vary, but this pastry should generally be put into a hot oven (425 F, Gas mark 6-7).

RICH SHORT CRUST PASTRY

This is made in exactly the same way, but for 8 oz of flour you should use 3 oz of butter and 3 oz of margarine; and also add the yolk of an egg in place of some cold water.

SWEET SHORT CRUST

Either of these two pastry recipes can be sweetened by simply adding a teaspoon of castor sugar and mixing well in at the 'breadcrumbs' stage.

BAKING BLIND

Not, as you might imagine, Shughie McFee trying to make a cake at midnight on Hogmanay . . . ! Some recipes require that the pastry case should be cooked before it is filled (in the case of custard tarts, flans, etc). To do this, line your flan-tin with pastry and prick with a fork at regular intervals all over. Cut a round of greaseproof paper slightly larger than the tin, and grease it. Put it on the pastry, greased side down, and then fill the pastry case with dried beans, dried peas or rice. Cook in a hot oven (450 F, Gas mark 8) for about a quarter of an hour.

PACKED LUNCHES
AND PICNICS

Our guests at Crossroads are not only busy travellers breaking their journey and refreshing themselves conveniently in the very heart of the country outside England's second largest city. Some come as delegates to big international conferences; some make the Motel their base when watching a cricket match at Edgbaston and some have discovered the beautiful towns and countryside which are within easy reach. They visit Coventry Cathedral and the nearby Belgrade Theatre built from wood donated by Yugoslavia after the war. They go walking in the Lickey Hills, or discover the beauty of Lichfield's three-spire Cathedral and, of course, they go to Stratford-upon-Avon. It is because of these sightseeing guests that Crossroads has gained a reputation for its box lunches and picnics.

Meg has considerable experience in this field. Like many mothers, she had the eternal problem of Jill and Sandy not liking school lunches and preferring to take sandwiches. Jill had the usual adolescent agonies about puppy fat. Meg was equally determined that no active, growing schoolgirl should exist on nothing but a lettuce leaf so she found her ingenuity taxed to the limit in devising packed lunches that were both nourishing and varied. She found that her success in this respect gave her a head start when she decided to offer lunch boxes and picnics as one of the facilities on offer at the Motel.

Bernard Booth agrees that there are four main requirements for such a meal. It should be well-balanced to provide adequate nourishment and most important it should be appetising and interesting. Attractive presentation makes the world of difference. Lastly it should be conveniently packed and easy to eat.

Packed meals are now much easier to transport with the advent of sealed plastic boxes and the various wraps make it simple to keep the food fresh. (Additionally, the Motel provides insulated boxes and flasks for hot or cold food and drink.)

A refreshing and appetising starter for a picnic meal is the following soup:

ICED CARROT AND ORANGE SOUP

1 lb new carrots	juice of 4 oranges and the
1 medium onion, sliced	finely grated rind of
1 oz butter	1 orange
1½ pints chicken stock	⅓ pint single cream
salt	chopped chives or spring
1 level teaspoon sugar	onion tops for
	decoration

Scrape and slice the carrots thinly. Melt the butter in a saucepan and add the carrots and onion. Fry gently until soft but not browned. Stir in the stock, salt, sugar and orange rind. Bring to the boil, stir, cover and simmer gently for one hour. Remove from the heat and pass through a sieve or blend in the liquidiser to make a puree. Add the strained orange juice and cream. Cool then chill for at least three hours. Serve sprinkled with chopped chives or spring onion tops. These should be taken in a separate container if the soup is to be served at a picnic.

Hugh Mortimer is passionately fond of kippers and here is one recipe which may be served hot or cold, and so is ideal for picnics.

KIPPER QUICHE

a shortcrust pastry case	2 teaspoons French
pair of kippers	mustard
½ pint double cream	grated nutmeg
2 large eggs	salt, pepper and lemon juice

Bake the kippers sealed in foil in a pre-heated oven at 350 F,
Gas mark 4, for thirty minutes. Line a flan dish with the
pastry and bake blind at the top of the same oven for 10
minutes.

Skin and bone the kippers carefully, flake the flesh and put
it into the pastry case with a little lemon juice squeezed over
it. Whisk all the remaining ingredients together, pour the
mixture into the flan, and put it in the centre of the oven.
Bake for 35-40 minutes until the filling has risen slightly and
is gold in colour.

PISSALADIERE

Hugh's son Anthony discovered Pissaladiere when on holiday in France. It is closely related to pizza and can be made
with a leavened pizza dough. However, the following recipe
may be more popular as the lining is lighter and less stodgy.

8 oz flaky pastry	a little olive oil
4 oz soft chopped fried onion	12 black stoned and halved olives
1 tin anchovy fillets	black pepper

Line a flan dish or sandwich tin with the flaky pastry.
Spread the onions in the dish and season with pepper. Make
a trellis on top of this with the anchovy strips and put one
olive in each square. Sprinkle lightly with olive oil and bake
in a fairly hot oven (375 F, Gas mark 5) for 25 minutes.

Pasties are a convenient way to prepare food for a box
lunch. They may be made in puff or shortcrust pastry and
are particularly good in cheese shortcrust. This is made like
ordinary shortcrust (see page 161) and the ingredients for
1 lb are as follows: 6 oz flour, 4 oz grated cheese, 2 egg yolks,
3 oz butter, salt, cayenne pepper, and a little water.

This first recipe was one of Paul Stevens' favourites and he
still makes it for the guests in his hotel in Guernsey.

CHEESE AND HADDOCK TRICORNES

8 oz cheese shortcrust	2 oz grated Parmesan cheese
6 oz cooked smoked	cayenne pepper
haddock	1 tablespoon milk
2 oz butter	1 egg

Mash all the ingredients except the pastry together well. Roll out the pastry and cut into 4″ circles. Put a spoonful of the mixture into the centre of each circle and pinch the edges up in three places to make the shape of a three cornered hat. Seal and brush with beaten egg to which a little salt has been added. Bake in hot oven (450 F, Gas mark 8) for 10 to 15 minutes.

FISH ENVELOPES

Another tasty and simple way of using up fish is Fish Envelopes.

8 oz puff pastry	1 tablespoon minced parsley
8 oz cooked white fish	2 tablespoons white sauce

Roll out the pastry and cut into 6″ squares. Place the fish, sauce and parsley mixture in the centre of the squares. Fold in the four corners (like an envelope) then seal and glaze with egg and bake at 425 F, Gas mark 7), for 10 to 15 minutes.

Finally, here is another filling which is popular with our Crossroads guests.

SAVOURY PASTY

2 chopped hardboiled eggs	3 tablespoons white sauce
6 oz ham, chopped	to bind the above
¼ lb chopped cooked onion	ingredients together
2 oz grated cheese	pepper and salt
¼ lb skinned, sliced	
tomatoes	

We usually make this pasty with shortcrust pastry.

Pies are a useful standby for picnics. They can be prepared well in advance, look attractive and appetizing and are easy to pack. Here are some of our Crossroads specialities – beginning with:

MR BOOTH'S BEEF PIE

8 oz shortcrust pastry	4 oz grated cheese
5 oz chopped corned beef	3 eggs
1 grated onion	salt and pepper

Grease a sandwich tin or flan dish and line with the pastry, leaving sufficient to make a cover for the pie. Put layers of corned beef, onions and grated cheese in the pie, seasoning well. Pour beaten egg over this mixture, cover with remaining pastry (sealing well with beaten egg), brush top with a little more egg and bake in a moderate oven (375 F, Gas mark 5) for 25 minutes. This may be served hot but for picnics serve it cold with a green salad.

RAISED BACON AND EGG PIE

hot water crust pastry:	3 hardboiled eggs
1 lb plain flour	2 tablespoons chopped
2 level teaspoons salt	parsley
4 oz lard	2 tablespoons tomato paste
7 fluid oz water	freshly ground black
	pepper
Filling:	½ pint aspic jelly
2 lb boiling bacon	
1 beaten egg	

Sieve flour and salt into a bowl. Boil water and lard together. Pour into flour and mix thoroughly. Grease well a 7″ round cake tin. Take three quarters of the pastry and mould it into the tin to give an even covering.

Mince half the bacon and mix with the beaten egg, tomato paste, parsley and black pepper. Line the pastry with this. Fill the centre with remaining bacon, chopped, and 2 chopped hardboiled eggs. Put a whole egg in the centre. Cover with rest of pastry and decorate. Bake at 425 F, Gas mark 7 for 30 minutes then reduce heat to 350 F, Gas mark 4 for a further 15 minutes. Allow to cool before filling (through hole in lid) with aspic jelly.

FARMHOUSE PIE

Here is a recipe that has been handed down for many generations in Granny Fraser's family.

For the pastry you will need a savoury shortcrust which is an ordinary shortcrust (see page 161) to which you add celery salt, garlic salt, mixed herbs and mustard.

2 *chopped onions*	**or** *half cooked chicken and*
3 *large tomatoes, skinned*	*half lambs' tongues*
and chopped	2 *oz butter*
1 *lb diced cooked lambs'*	*pepper and salt*
tongues (the tinned	1 *good tablespoon sweet*
variety will do very well)	*pickle*

Grease a two pound loaf tin and line with pastry, leaving sufficient over for a lid. Fry the onions and tomatoes in the butter until soft then blend in the meat. Season well and then add the sweet pickle. Fill the pie tin. Cover pie with pastry lid, cut hole to allow steam to escape, decorate with pastry leaves or triangles and brush with a little beaten egg for glaze. Bake in the centre of a hot oven (450 F, Gas mark 8) for 20 minutes then lower to very moderate (325 F, Gas mark 3) for a further 20 minutes.

POULET PAIN

And now a pie for a really special occasion. It is not really too costly, though a whole bottle of hock may sound extravagant; you can equally well use a bottle of Yugoslav Riesling which would be much cheaper.

Meg and Hugh were sent two tickets for Glyndebourne Opera by one of the Crossroads guests. It is a tradition that the opera-goers all wear evening dress (although it starts at about tea-time) and that they take a picnic supper to eat in the beautiful Sussex gardens during one of the long intervals between acts. The following dish is what Meg and Hugh chose to take with them and it was perfect for the occasion. Cut off the top side of a large, fresh sandwich loaf and remove the inside so that you have a hollow crusty case. Next cut a 3 lb roasting chicken into 9 pieces (2 legs, each broken in two at the joint, 2 wings and the breast cut across into 3 pieces). Season these pieces well and rub them lightly with flour. Heat 1 oz of butter and 1 oz of lard in a frying pan: add the chicken pieces and fry them for 5-6 minutes without letting them brown. Transfer the pieces to a saucepan and add 1 pint of hock (or Riesling), a carrot cut into four, an onion studded with two cloves, a bay leaf, a sprig of thyme, a stick of celery and a sprinkling of salt and pepper. Simmer for 35 minutes then add 1 oz gelatine crystals which have been previously dissolved in half a cup of hot water. Simmer for a further five minutes, stirring continuously. Now remove the chicken pieces from the bones, and keep them on one side. Pour the stock through a sieve, then remove vegetables and put back into the saucepan.

Whisk together 2 yolks of egg and 1 cup of double cream in a basin, adding one cup of the hot stock as you do so. Add this mixture to the rest of the hot stock and continue whisking over a low heat. When the stock has thickened, leave it to cool for about 15 minutes or so before pouring it over the chicken. Finally put the chicken and sauce inside the loaf and leave it to set in the refrigerator. Decorate the top with a pattern of triangles of ham and glaze with aspic jelly. Cover with the crust that you cut off and serve cold, in slices.

The simplest box lunch consists of a chicken-leg, some salad, such as lettuce and tomato, and fresh fruit. However, here is a tip from Bernard; don't dress the salad until you are ready to eat. Get the salad really well chilled in your refrigerator before putting the ingredients into an insulated box, if possible, and take your favourite dressing in a separate container.

Here are five recipes from the Motel kitchen which make easy-to-handle meals.

FRIED CHICKEN DRUMSTICKS

Skin the drumsticks. Roll them in well seasoned flour, then in beaten egg and finally in breadcrumbs. (These should be home made from fried white bread.) Fry until cooked, crisp and golden. Drain them on absorbent paper before wrapping them in greaseproof paper and sealing in aluminium foil.

SALAMI CHICKEN

Cut a slit along the side of the drumstick and loosen the flesh round the bone. Put two slices of salami round the bone and rejoin the flesh with cocktail sticks. Then cook as in the recipe above.

SCOTCH EGGS

4 *hardboiled eggs*	*flour*
3 *oz grated Cheddar cheese*	*beaten egg*
12 *oz sausage meat*	*breadcrumbs*

Cut the eggs in half and carefully scoop out the yolks. Mix these well with the grated cheese and stuff back into the whites. Re-form the four eggs and cover with sausage meat. Roll each Scotch egg in flour, then egg and finally bread-crumbs. Fry until crisp and brown.

CORNED BEEFBURGERS

3 rashers of bacon
1 oz cooking fat
1 grated onion
¼ lb mushrooms, chopped

12 oz corned beef
3 oz fresh breadcrumbs
½ teaspoon mixed herbs
pepper, salt, potato crisis

Chop the bacon finely and fry it in the fat until it is almost crisp. Add the onion and mushrooms and cook until onion has softened. Mix in the corned beef, breadcrumbs, herbs and seasoning and cook for a little longer. Make into eight flat cakes and coat with crushed potato crisps. Chill well and serve in soft buttered baps.

HOLIDAY CHEESE BALLS

1 packet Black Diamond
   Cheddar cheese

sufficient beer to combine
   to make a paste

Let cheese warm to room temperature. Thoroughly blend with the beer in a blender. Cool mixture in refrigerator until firm enough to form into balls. Roll cheese balls in either chopped nuts, finely ground carrots, parsley or paprika. Wrap in foil and put in freezer until ready to serve – perhaps on a large cabbage leaf.

French loaves are readily obtainable almost everywhere in Britain now and they form the basis of some tasty picnic dishes – acting as they do as a cross between a pastry-cased pie and a sandwich. Here are four ways we treat them at Crossroads.

FRENCH LOAF OMELETTE

Slice the loaf lengthways, about a quarter of the way down from the brown crust. Scoop out the crumb. You should now have a container with a lid.

Spread the inside with a mixture of butter and made mustard then line it with sliced ham. Make a large omelette

(5-6 eggs), fold it in the usual way and slide it into the loaf. Cover with more ham and replace the lid. Wrap tightly in foil and serve in slices when needed.

STUFFED FRENCH LOAF I
Cream together 2 oz butter, 2 teaspoons of made mustard and two tablespoons of tomato ketchup. Add one teaspoon chopped gherkin and one or two tablespoons of chopped spring onion or chives. Mix all this with ¾ lb of liver sausage or minced cooked meat. Split the loaves, butter and fill.

STUFFED FRENCH LOAF II

5 *sticks celery, peeled and chopped*	*milk*
butter	*salt and freshly ground pepper*
4 *oz cream cheese*	

Mix all these ingredients thoroughly and pile into loaf.

PAIN BAGNIA
This is the French equivalent of the English ploughman's lunch. It is a peasant dish from the South of France where it is accompanied superbly by the rich red wine of Provence. This recipe was given to David Hunter when he was on holiday there. It is strongly flavoured and he gives this warning – this is not the food for a romantic picnic unless *both* of you eat it!

1 *French loaf*	2 *tablespoons olive oil*
1 *clove of garlic, crushed*	1 *teaspoon lemon juice or vinegar*
10 *stoned olives*	
2 *tomatoes*	*a few cooked French beans*
3 *or 4 anchovies*	

Chop the garlic, olives, pepper, tomatoes and anchovies together finely (an Autochop is ideal for this) and moisten with oil and lemon juice to make a thick paste. Spread this

172

thickly on the loaf which has been cut in half lengthways. Sprinkle on a few cooked beans and press the halves together, weighting them down slightly. Chill, and wrap closely in foil. Cut into thick slices when serving.

SANDWICHES

When the Earl of Sandwich invented a way of taking nourishment without being distracted or disturbed at the gaming tables, he could have had no idea of the part his brainchild would play in our lives today. More and more people in all walks of life forego lunch for the sake of time and economy and take a sandwich or two at the nearest inn or sandwich bar to their place of work. At Crossroads Motel we have a busy lunch trade in sandwiches and these are Jane Smith's particular responsibility. She offers the following tips for sandwich making:

★As bread is at least half the sandwich, always use the best.

★Be generous with butter. It keeps the bread moist and prevents soft fillings making it soggy.

★It is nearly always better to pound or mince the ingredients finely than to chop them coarsely or untidily as it makes easier eating.

★Spread to the edge of the sandwich to avoid a dull first bite.

★For picnics, leave the crusts on to prevent the edges drying or curling.

★Allow a minimum of two rounds per person.

Here are three of Jane's special spreads which have proved popular with her customers.

BLUE CHEESE SPREAD

$\frac{1}{4}$ *lb blue cheese* (*Danish Blue or Roquefort*)	*2 tablespoons mayonnaise*
6 oz cream cheese	*2 tablespoons crisp diced bacon*

Mix the cheeses and mayonnaise together well, before adding the bacon.

173

CHEESE AND ORANGE SPREAD

4 oz cream cheese
2 tablespoons preserved
    ginger, finely chopped
2 teaspoons grated orange
    rind
3 tablespoons orange juice

Beat the first three ingredients until smooth before adding the orange juice.

AVOCADO SPREAD

4 oz mashed avocado
2 teaspoons minced onion
1 tablespoon lemon juice
1 tablespoon mayonnaise
a dash of Worcester sauce

Combine all the ingredients and beat to a smooth cream.

The combination of sandwich fillings are limitless and offer great scope for the imagination. However here are some of Crossroads' proven favourites:

Meat and Poultry
Liver sausage and cucumber
Liver sausage and cream cheese
Minced liver and bacon
Chopped mutton and mint jelly
Chopped beef and horseradish
Beef gherkin
Beef, grated beetroot and horseradish
Bacon and scrambled egg
Chopped chicken with mayonnaise
Minced turkey and cranberry sauce

Fish
Kipper and mustard
Crab, mayonnaise and capers or cucumber
White fish and pickled walnuts
Salmon and cucumber
Smoked salmon with cucumber and tomato sauce

Shrimps or prawns with mayonnaise
Smoked cod's roe with tomato, lettuce and tomato sauce
Prawn, celery, apple and tomato chutney
Smoked haddock and horseradish sauce
Tuna fish and grapefruit

Egg
Scrambled egg and chives
Scrambled egg and cress
Scrambled egg, cream cheese and chives
Chopped hardboiled eggs with butter and French dressing
Chopped hardboiled eggs with anchovy and watercress

Cheese
Grated cheese and chopped olives or gherkins
Grated cheese and mustard with sharp fruit sauce
Grated cheese and chutney
Grated cheese and grated onion
Grated cheese and apple, lemon juice and chutney
Cream cheese and pineapple
Cream cheese and chopped green peppers
Cream cheese and chopped nuts, lemon juice
Cream cheese and parsley
Cream cheese and shrimps

Vegetable
Grated raw cabbage, mayonnaise and grated horseradish
Grated raw carrot, celery and mayonnaise
Grated raw carrot and chutney
Anchovy butter with chopped watercress
Grated carrot, peanut butter and mayonnaise
Raw mushrooms, tomato and parsley
Apple, grated onion and mayonnaise
Mashed cooked peas, cream and mint

Sweet
Minced dates, walnuts and cream
Bananas, lemon, sugar and grated chocolate

Peanut butter, dates and honey

Crystallised ginger with whipped cream, lemon juice and sugar

Apple, nutmeg and brown sugar

Chopped nuts, honey and orange juice

SANDWICH CAKE

It seems fitting to end this chapter with Jane Smith's show-piece – Sandwich Cake. This is really a special occasion cake and is perfect for a birthday picnic or tea.

To make it you will need two sandwich loaves of similar size; one white and one brown. These you must slice carefully, lengthways, from the bottom to the top. Discard the top and bottom crusts and take a slice and butter it on one side only. You then take a slice of another colour and butter it on both sides. You continue to do this in alternate coloured bread until you come to your top slice which is buttered on the underside only.

Here are some suitable fillings, each to be put in separate layers:

I   Chopped ham
    Crisp bacon and sweet red pepper
    Hardboiled egg yolks
    Cream cheese
    Watercress

II Salmon
    Cucumber
    Cream cheese
    Egg

Alternate your fillings to make the colour combinations as attractive as possible.

When the sandwich cake has reached the required size, cut off the crusts with a sharp knife to leave a tidy rectangular shape. Now, with a knife you 'ice' the 'cake' with cream cheese; you will need $\frac{3}{4}$-1 lb to do this. You may then colour some cream cheese and with an icing nozzle decorate your sandwich cake in any way that you like.

Put the cake in a refrigerator for 3-4 hours before serving by cutting slices as you would with an ordinary loaf of bread – it will cause quite a sensation!

THE PROFESSIONAL TOUCH—
by Meg

Over the years Meg has kept a book of handy tips which she has collected from the various Motel chefs. She calls it her Disaster Manual. Many of these professional hints have proved useful to Meg in emergencies when entertaining privately and she decided to pass them on to us for inclusion in this book.

1. When boiling potatoes, if they overcook and become 'mashy', sprinkle some crisp fried onions over the top. It adds to the appearance and taste.

2. When adding milk to a sauce, if it looks as if it is going to curdle, add a teaspoon of flour and continue stirring.

3. If you have added too many herbs to a dish (ie Cottage Pie), to eliminate the strong flavour soak some breadcrumbs in milk, or fry some breadcrumbs and mix in.

4. If you find you have only one carton of single cream and this is not enough, whip an egg white with a pinch of salt and fold in. This will double the quantity.

5. When a recipe calls for a raw egg to be added to a soup, do not put the egg straight into the soup – this makes it separate when cooked and little white pieces will float in it. Instead, whip the egg first in a basin, add a small amount of soup to the whipped egg and stir and then pour the mixture into the saucepan of soup.

6. If you discover the sides of a cake have burnt, take the finest side of a grater and rub gently up and down the sides. This will remove all burnt crumbs.

7. When a fresh lettuce has wilted, plunge it into hot water, shake well and then plunge it into ice cold water to which a drop of vinegar has been added. Then return the lettuce to the crisper compartment of the fridge and it will be as good as new.

8. When frying onions to a golden brown and it appears they are not going the right colour, sprinkle some sugar on them. This will brown and crisp them but will not sweeten the onions in any way.

9. If you find it difficult to get cakes out of a tin, wrap the tin in a warm tea towel and this will loosen the cake from the sides.

10. When cooking icing sugar to make a glaze, add a few drops of vinegar and this will prevent the icing sugar crystallising.

11. If extra guests should turn up unexpectedly and you have not got enough meat for hamburgers, add some apple sauce and some grated cheese. This gives a lovely flavour and makes meat go further.

12. When cooking with butter always add a small amount of oil to prevent the butter browning.

13. When grilling, if the fat splutters or a smoky haze rises from the grill, always put some stale bread under the grid of the grill. This will absorb the fat and prevent the spluttering.

14. Sometimes, with the advent of North Sea Gas, one finds the jets too powerful for simmering. Alternatively the jet goes out if put on too low. Both these dangers can be avoided by using an asbestos mat and turning the gas a little higher. This prevents burning and also prevents the gas from going out.

15. When making a lemon sauce, if you do not wish to use and squeeze all your lemon, cut a wedge and put it on the end of a fork; then stir the sauce with this instead of a wooden spoon. This saves lemon without minimising the flavour.

16. When making omelettes do not add salt to the beaten egg until *just before* cooking as otherwise it makes the egg watery.

17. To prevent rice boiling over, add a knob of butter.

18. When cooking potatoes always add a knob of butter and

a piece of lemon peel. This adds to the flavour and they keep their colour.

19. When cooking cauliflower always add a spot of milk to keep its colour white and a small crust of bread to prevent the smell pervading the house.

20. Crisis batter! When you want to make a batter and you find there are no eggs in the house, use beer as a substitute and you will find you have a lovely crisp batter.

21. When friends come round unexpectedly and all you have in the fridge is a frozen chicken – to defrost with maximum speed soak it (in its plastic bag) in salt water.

22. If you have any roast potatoes left over – don't throw them away. You can use them for another meal by putting them in warm water, drying them well with absorbent paper, then brushing with oil and putting them in a moderate oven. Hey presto! Fresh roast potatoes!

23. Use evaporated milk instead of fresh when making soups and sauces – the consistency is creamier.

24. To cut bread really thin for dainty sandwiches, always warm the knife first. This gives a sharp, clean and very thin slice.

25. Never wash an omelette pan. Rub it with some kitchen paper after use and this will ensure that future omelettes never stick.

Very old friends of the family will remember that Meg's first husband – Charles Richardson – was an artist; and perhaps it was from Charles that Meg acquired her eye for layout and colour. As a catering expert, she is very much aware of the importance of presentation where food is concerned – and so we have decided to close the book by giving Meg herself –

THE LAST WORD

Meg says:

'It seems to me that the *look* of food is almost as important as the taste. If a meal looks immediately attractive, the battle is practically won before you begin. Set those old gastric juices to work the moment your guests see the dishes laid out on the table, and you can sit back and wait for the compliments to start rolling in!

'In running a professional restaurant, we're continually on the lookout for new ways to make our menus attractive; and here are a few hints I've learned over the years ...

'Fireproof dishes, whether they're in glass or earthenware, are very suitable for serving straight from the oven. The food is always bubbling hot, and you don't have the problem of juggling the contents into serving-dishes – with the possible risk of the food disintegrating on the way. The only disadvantage to these ovenproof dishes is that they do collect dark stains where food or gravy burns on the sides. These can easily be removed with a damp cloth dipped in a little salt. Perhaps the ideal cook-and-serve dish is a copper pan, which can be warmed over direct heat.

'Aim at covering the guest's plate evenly, with no blank spaces between the items of food. Try the effect of dividing your main vegetable into two, with half on each side of the plate, balancing these with smaller heaps of the other vegetables dotted around. Don't serve more than one green vegetable at any meal (that sounds obvious, but it's awfully easy to do if you don't "see" the effect in your mind's eye – and you find you've ended up with spring greens *and* frozen peas). An all-white dish should be avoided as well; chicken or veal in a white sauce, with mashed potatoes and leeks, for instance.

'Add dashes of colour by using tiny amounts of additional vegetable for garnishing; sliced carrot, red cabbage, sprigs of parsley, tomatoes, mushrooms or croutons (diced fried bread) are all useful in this way – and so are watercress, shredded horseradish, radish "roses" and sliced gherkins. Cucumber and grapes are excellent with fish; and of course red-currant jelly or mint sauce are the classic accompaniments for lamb. Orange slices with fish, or lemon wedges

182

with chicken, both enhance their appearance; and don't neglect the addition of a few shrimps to any white fish. Onions are versatile, served chopped and raw, or fried in rings – and spring onions too can be very useful.

'As for table decoration . . . one of the loveliest colour-schemes I ever saw, in the middle of winter when cut flowers were few and far between, was based on a flat wicker basket filled with brazil nuts and shining tangerines, making a brilliant splash of colour against the dark polished wood of the table. The tones were carried through with brown earthenware dishes and orange napkins, and the effect was warm and glowing, like an open log fire.

'Another unusual theme for a table decoration is "Oranges and Lemons" – the fresh, scrubbed fruit piled in a rough pyramid, surrounded by glossy dark-green leaves from your garden.

'Nightlights, set in a shallow dish of water, with flower-heads (dahlias or chrysanthemums perhaps) floating on the water around them, can look very effective. But any extra source of light adds excitement to a table-setting. If you can contrive it, bring the main overhead light down low, with a dark shade (to prevent your guests from being dazzled) to cast a pool of light on the tabletop. If this can't be managed, try to avoid the overhead light altogether, and bring a small lamp on to the centre of the dinner-table, with a softly-coloured shade.

'Candles, too, are always a sure-fire ingredient for success – especially if you make a centrepiece in which candles sit among a garland of flowers. If you have one of those spiky flower-holders, try sticking tall thin candles on two or three of the spikes – though you must take care to keep the flowers well below the level of the flames.

'For the very special celebration, a fingerbowl by the side of each lady's plate, with one rose floating in it, will look quite charming – and how about a clear glass vase filled with chocolates and mints (some wrapped in brightly-coloured tinfoil) at the coffee stage of the meal? All these things help to add the final touch of glamour, and turn an everyday meal into an occasion.

'After which it only remains for me to say – on behalf of all your friends on the staff of the Crossroads Motel –

' "Bon appetit! . . . and we hope that you enjoy your meal." '

INDEX TO RECIPES

INDEX TO RECIPES

188

FILMS & TV

0352　Star

30006X	**THE MAKING OF KING KONG** B. Bahrenburg	60p*
398957	**THE MARRIAGE RING ("COUPLES")** Paddy Kitchen & Dulan Barber	60p
397276	**MURDER BY DEATH** H. R. F. Keating	60p*
398825	**McCOY: THE BIG RIP-OFF** Sam Stewart	50p*
398035	**PAUL NEWMAN** Michael Kerbel	75p
397470	**ODE TO BILLY JOE** Herman Raucher	60p*'
398191	**THE ROCKFORD FILES** Mike Jahn	50p*
397373	**THE SCARLET BUCCANEER** D. R. Benson	60p*
398442	**THE SIX MILLION DOLLAR MAN 3: THE RESCUE OF ATHENA ONE** Mike Jahn	45p*
398647	**THE SIX MILLION DOLLAR MAN 4: PILOT ERROR** Jay Barbree	50p*
396490	**SIX MILLION DOLLAR MAN 5: THE SECRET OF BIGFOOT** Mike Jahn	60p
396652	**SPACE 1999: (No. 2) MIND BREAKS OF SPACE** Michael Butterworth	60p
396660	**SPACE 1999 (No. 1) PLANETS OF PERIL** Michael Butterworth	60p
398531	**SPANISH FLY** Madelaine Duke	50p
398817	**SWITCH** Mike Jahn	50p*
398051	**THE ULTIMATE WARRIOR** Bill S. Ballinger	50p*

0426　Tandem

180240	**AT THE EARTH'S CORE** Edgar Rice Burroughs	50p
180321	**THE LAND THAT TIME FORGOT** Edgar Rice Burroughs	50p
164164	**LENNY** Valerie Kohler Smith	50p*
16184X	**ONEDIN LINE: THE HIGH SEAS** Cyril Abraham	60p
132661	**ONEDIN LINE: THE IRON SHIPS**	60p
168542	**SHAMPOO** Robert Alley	50p

*Not for sale in Canada.

Wyndham Books are obtainable from many booksellers and newsagents. If you have any difficulty please send purchase price plus postage on the scale below to:

Wyndham Cash Sales,
44 Hill Street
London W1X 8LB

OR

Star Book Service,
G.P.O. Box 29,
Douglas,
Isle of Man,
British Isles

While every effort is made to keep prices low, it is sometimes necessary to increase prices at short notice. Wyndham Books reserve the right to show new retail prices on covers which may differ from those advertised in the text or elsewhere.

Postage and Packing Rate
U.K. & Eire
One book 15p plus 7p per copy for each additional book ordered to a maximum charge of 57p.

These charges are subject to Post Office charge fluctuations.